© Editions du Regard, Paris, 1996. © A.D.A.G.P., Paris, 1996.
© S.P.A.D.E.M., Paris, 1996.
Introduction: Philippe Morane
Photography: Jacques Boulay, Patricia Canino and Karine Veyrunes
Iconography: Françoise Pace
Design: Léo Thieck

© 1998 for this edition
Könemann Verlagsgesellschaft mbH
Bonner Str. 126
D - 50968 Köln

Translation from French: Dr. John Crook
Editor of English-language edition: Sharon Herson
Typesetting: Goodfellow & Egan
Production manager: Detlev Schaper
Assistant: Nicola Leurs
Printing and binding: Leefung Asco-Printers, China

ISBN 3-8290-1066-4

10 9 8 7 6 5 4 3 2 1

ERIC DESCHODT
PHILIPPE MORANE

The Cigar

INTRODUCTION: PHILIPPE MORANE

PHOTOGRAPHS:
JACQUES BOULAY - PATRICIA CANINO
KARINE VEYRUNES

ILLUSTRATIONS: FRANÇOISE PACE

KÖNEMANN

CONTENTS

Facing page: Montecristo A (*especial*) cigars.

INTRODUCTION

*C*uba occupies first place in this book for three reasons. First, it was there that Columbus discovered the cigar, at the same time as tobacco. Second, its tobaccos were from the outset recognized as superior to all others, and this opinion has not changed in five hundred years. Finally, in Cuba tobacco has a history inextricably linked with that of the island, and it is a unique case. Cuba is the only country whose national emblem could be tobacco—the whole plant, its leaf, or its flower— just like the maple leaf for Canada or the fleur-de-lis for royal France. At the end of the last century, during the War of Independence, in which the *tabaqueros* formed the spearhead, it appeared on patriot flags in revolt against Spain. Nearer our time, Che Guevara stated, without fear of contradiction: "Tobacco is ours."

"Ours" means universal, but it is important to analyze the evolution of the cigar smoker and the opinion in which he was held by society in the 19th and 20th centuries. A symbol of social success and of elegance in the nineteenth century, he was nevertheless most often represented in the press—and especially in satirical magazines— as a self-satisfied boss, in shirtsleeves, thumbs tugging at his suspenders, the symbol of the triumph of capitalism, personal success, and the exploitation of the people.

Then Havana tobacco was banned in the United States and became scarce in Europe. This increased both the attraction of *puro* cigars and the number of enthusiasts who began to organize themselves. Specialist magazines appeared: *Cigar Aficionado* in the United States, *L'Amateur du cigare* in France, *Épicure* in Spain, and so on. Numerous smoking clubs were founded. Smoking-rooms multiplied in restaurants, bars, and big hotels. At the same time, festivals and cigar evenings attracted an increasing number of enthusiasts. For a cigar smoker, essentially a passionate type, the ban could only reinforce his passion. Smoking cigars is a pleasure but also a sign of openness: smokers like to share their sensual delights.

Perhaps Stéphane Mallarmé, the 19th-century symbolist poet and a great cigar lover, could be considered a precursor of this attitude. Replying to a series of questions by Marcel Proust, he stated straight off:

"Your dream of happiness?"   *"Dreaming."*

"Your worst misfortune?"   *"Not to light up my cigar."*

Even when our passion is spent, it is far from being extinguished.

PHILIPPE MORANE

Preceding pages: Violeta holds out a cigar to a flame being extended to her.

Facing page: Bolívar cigar box, Havana, Cuba.

*A*ll desires end in disillusion, all possessions are a disappointment, all pleasures are a mixed blessing. Love implies a partner (onanism is not love), alcohol leads to a hangover, war to death, gambling to ruin, greediness to obesity. There are no exceptions. In order to go sailing you need a boat; to hunt, a gun—or a horse and hounds. The pleasures of collecting are the most frustrating of all (the devotee is always lacking a Titian or a Rothko). Making one's fortune is never-ending: the nearer you get to your goal, the further away it is.

Objects of pure sensual delight are rare in this world. Even the greatest wines— perish the thought—can serve to quench one's thirst, utilitarian infamy. But the only use of the cigar is for smoking, and smoking is a pleasure, cigar smoking the supreme pleasure.

Cigars favor isolation as much as contact. You light one up to escape the world and yourself as well as to bring it closer. Its smoke both isolates and brings closer; it is both a mask and a link. It is an instrument of separation as well as of sharing. One can only smoke in peace, but smoking also spreads peace. What statesman can claim as much without lying?

The invention of the cigar surpasses all the others because it is free. Its simplicity makes it the equal in nobility to the highest products of the human mind. Entirely natural, it involves no artifice. The four elements—earth, air, fire, and water—and the hand of man, without any intermediary apart from the cigar roller's guillotine, intervene alone in its development, then in the flourishing which is its final burning. A natural product, the cigar is homogeneous and coherent: tobacco in tobacco, nothing but tobacco. Real cigars escape machinery. They come into contact only with the roller's hand, the wood of their boxes, the hand and lips of the smoker, before being transmuted into stimulating and consoling smoke.

Tobacco quickly conquered the world, but the expansion of the cigar was very slow; a difference which is even more troubling since the cigar was the first way of smoking tobacco. The pipe is dated, the cigarette quite recent, while the cigar goes back to the dawn of time. We do not know for how many thousands of years it helped its inventors, the American Indians, to overcome the difficulties of life.

Facing page: Maria, daughter of Yemaya, daughter of the sea and queen of Havana, 1995.

Following page: Vignette with a tropical emphasis proclaims: "Great manufacturer of fine tobacco—exquisite."

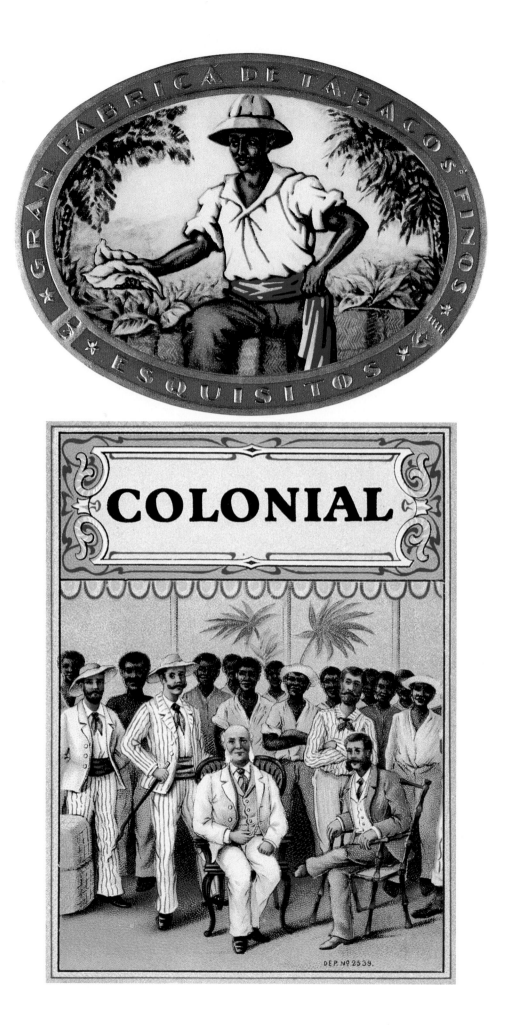

CHAPTER
I

A HISTORY

Christopher Columbus discovered the cigar, together with the New World, in 1492. Whether the latter discovery was a good thing or not is perhaps an open question, but that of the cigar was one of the most outstandingly propitious events in the history of the human race. Its discovery alone justified that of the continent. The formation of this marvelous link whereby the Old World depended on the New would wipe out everything else: the impudence of the conquest, the excesses of the conquerors, the weaknesses of the conquered. Unless, that is, the gift of the cigar, more precious than Aztec or Inca gold, rendered quite unforgivable Europe's violence toward the native Americans —however involuntary it may have been.

Christopher Columbus, sailing toward the west, knew he was traveling toward unknown lands. He did not doubt that he would discover wonderfully strange things there. The cigar was the first. On 4 November 1492, Rodrigo de Jerez and Luis de Torres disembarked in Cuba, envoys of the admiral and the first white men to set foot in the new paradise. When they returned on board the admiral wrote:

All portraits of Christopher Columbus are imaginary. For all that, it was he who discovered tobacco and America.

"These envoys met a great number of Indians, both men and women, who were holding a small piece of smoldering tinder with which to light certain herbs with which they perfume themselves, following their custom."

1493. Columbus had returned to Europe with his crews, and tobacco claimed its first martyr. While smoking in a Madrid street—smoking what is the question (one hopes it was a cigar, and this is plausible since pipes were unknown)—Luis de Torres was arrested by the Inquisition and condemned to ten years' imprisonment for sorcery. Ironically, the time would come when Spanish clergymen would have the best cigars in the world made for their sole use.

Amerigo Vespucci met Indians chewing tobacco on the island of Margarita, off the Venezuela coast. A letter by him dated 1507 is the first text in which the word tobacco appears. In 1519 Cortés arrived in Mexico; the Aztecs smoked pipes especially; these were perhaps cigar holders, for they were holding rolled-up tobacco leaves. In 1520 tobacco was circulating in a few Spanish ports—Seville, Cadiz,

Moguer, Cartagena—as well as Portuguese ones, such as Lisbon. In 1525, the year of Pavia, when François I was captured by the imperial forces, Jean d'Ango, a Dieppe shipbuilder and buccaneer, who two years previously had sent the Florentine Verrazano to North America, praised tobacco in his *Chanson des pilotes* [*Song of the Pilots*] in the following terms:

"Yesterday I met an old sailor and I drank a jug of Brittany wine with him. While drinking he suddenly pulled out of his wallet a white clay object which at first I thought was a schoolboy's inkhorn. You would have said it was an inkhorn with a long pipe and a small mouth; he filled the wide end with brown leaves which he had crushed in the palm of his hands, set fire to it by means of a tinderbox, and the very next moment, having put the pipe between his lips, he was blowing smoke out of his mouth, which I found quite astounding. He apprised me that the Portuguese had taught him this trick, which they had learned from Mexican Indians. He called it 'smoking' and said that this smoking sharpened up the mind and produced happy thoughts."

In 1530 tobacco served as currency for buying the first slaves on the African coast. The negroes would quickly start growing it. In 1535 Jacques Cartier and his ships were icebound in the St. Lawrence River. The Indians saved his crews from scurvy. We read as follows in his *Bref récit de la navigation faite dans les Isles du Canada* [*Short Account of Navigation in the Isles of Canada*]:

"They also possess a herb which they pile up in great heaps during the winter, which they hold in great estimation, the men alone using it as follows: they dry it in the sun and carry it in a little animal-skin pouch around their necks, together with a stone or horn funnel, then at any time of day they crush the said herb and put it in one end of the said funnel, then apply a coal to it and suck on the other end, so that their whole body is filled with smoke, so much so that it comes out of their mouth and nostrils as if from a chimney; they said that it keeps them healthy and warm. ... We tried out the aforementioned smoke, and having drawn it into our mouths felt that we had put ground pepper there, so hot it was."

The Dominican Bartolomé de Las Casas, author of *Breve Relación de la Destrucción de las Indias* [*A Very Brief Account of the Destruction of the Indies*], published in 1542 in order to denounce the brutalities of colonization, provided the first precise description of the cigar:

"They were dried herbs rolled up in a certain leaf, also dried, forming a kind of paper 'fusee' like children make for the feast of Pentecost. People lit them at one end, sucked the other, and absorbed the smoke by breathing it in. This smoke sent them to sleep and intoxicated them, as you might say, and prevented them, they claimed, from feeling sleepy. These 'fusees,' or whatever we may call them, they themselves called 'tabaccos.'…"

In 1550 a Brazilian festival was given at Rouen for Henry II and his wife, Catherine de Medici. It would be described the following year in a document entitled *The Entry of Henry II and Catherine de Medici into Rouen*. It notes, "And while all this was going on, behold, a band of savages arrived, known in their own language as 'tabagerres' according to their partialities." In 1554 tobacco was found in the gardens of present-day Belgium. In 1555 the Frenchman Villegagnon returned from Brazil. The Indians of the Rio de Janeiro region were smoking "cigars and rudimentary cigarettes" very similar to the "joints" of junkies (*Encyclopédie du tabac*).

Catherine de Medici, queen of France, by François Clouet. Tobacco helped calm her migraines, and she nearly gave it her name.

1556. André Thevet, a Cordelier monk and Villegagnon's companion, planted the first tobacco plants in France, in his Angoulême garden. The following year he published his *Singularités de la France Antarctique* [*Curiosities of Antarctic France*], in which the cigar crops up again:

"Another singularity of the herb which in their tongue they call 'petun,' which they usually carry on them because they consider it marvelously beneficial in several regards. It resembles our bugloss. Now, they carefully cultivate this herb and dry it in the shade in their little huts. The way they use it is as follows. Once it is dry, they wrap a certain quantity of this weed in a very large palm leaf, rolling it up into a candle's length, then they set fire to one end and inhale the smoke through their nose and mouth."

"It is salubrious, they say, for distilling and consuming the superfluous humors of the brain. More of it taken in this way alleviates hunger and thirst for a time. For this reason, they normally use it even when they are involved in everyday affairs; they take in this smoke and then talk; which they habitually do one after another while engaged in war, where it is found very useful. Women do not use it at all. True, if you take too much of this smoke or scent, it goes to your head and inebriates you like the fumes of a strong wine. The Christians who are now in those parts have become amazingly fond of this herb and its smell, even though at the outset its use is not without its dangers until you are used to it; for this smoke makes you perspire and feel faint, even to the point of falling unconscious—as I tried out for myself. That is less strange than it may seem, for other fruits may be found which offend the brain, however delicate and good to eat they may be."

These muscular natives, whose anatomy conforms to the canons of the School of Fontainebleau, are keeping up their spirits while hunting by smoking large fusees. From André Thevet's *Cosmographie universelle*, 1575.

A touching defense of tobacco, which no more harms the mind than many other excellent fruits. It did not protect Thevet from being accused, often plausibly, alas, of exaggeration or of storytelling pure and simple. Constantly ill during his stay in Brazil, he brought back only secondhand information, which he could not check out at all. His passion for the new herb earned him comparison, as a good Renaissance man, to Pliny, Appian, Herodotus. So what if tobacco went to one's head? According to Pliny, even pure water can do the same: "In Lyncestes there is a fountain whose water makes people drunk; similarly there is another in Paphlagonia." These countries seem all too fabulous to contemporary readers. Yet,

Pl. 60.

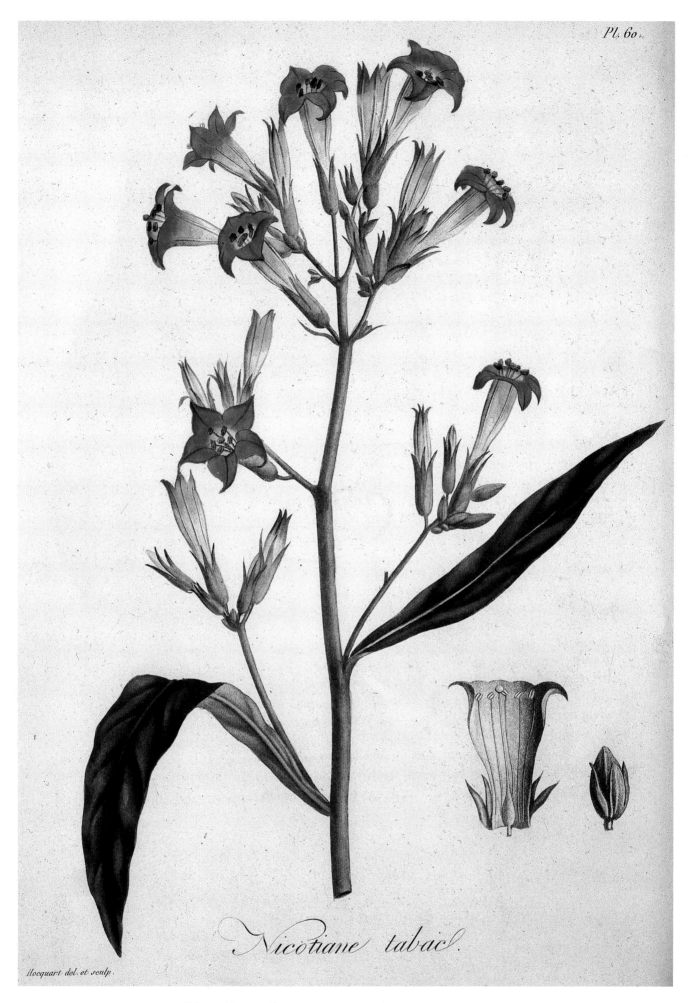

Nicotiane tabac.

Hocquart del. et sculp.

Tobacco. *Nicotiana tabacum* L. Joseph Roques, *Phytographie médicale*. Paris, 1921.

the Cordelier monk insisted: "If anyone wasn't content with our testimony, let him read Herodotus who, in Book II, mentions an African people who live on herbs alone." As for Appian, he "tells that the Parthians, shamed and banished from their country by Mark Anthony, lived on a certain plant which took away their memory, yet they still remained convinced that it nourished them well, despite the fact that they died within a short space of time. Which just goes to show how strange is the story we have to tell of tobacco."

DIGRESSIONS AND MISTRUST

A year after the publication of *Curiosities*, in 1558, Francisco Hernandez de Toledo, physician to Philip II of Spain, brought Mexican plants back to that country; though Thevet's account was largely confirmed by the Protestant minister Jean de Léry, the latter contradicted his papist rival in several important particulars. Having first, in his preface, accused the Cordelier of a host of foul deeds, Léry challenged the assertion that tobacco was restricted to men in Amazonia; women and children indulged just as much. Offering a cigar, he argued, was a sign of friendship.

His *Relation de voyage au Brésil* [*Account of a Voyage to Brazil*] would be published in 1576. Once again, he lays stress on the importance of tobacco to Indian beliefs. Smoking for them was not merely just a pleasure.

"I even noted that they often picked up a wooden cane four or five feet long, at the end of which there was dried tobacco which they had set alight; turning around and blowing its smoke on the other savages they said to them: 'In order to overcome your enemies, receive, all of you, the spirit of strength.'"

In 1560, a man from Nîmes, Jean Nicot, privy secretary to the king and Rapporteur of the Council of State, who officially had been sent to Lisbon to negotiate the marriage of the Infante Sebastian to Marguerite of Valois, daughter of Henri II and Catherine de Medici, and who was more seriously engaged in a mission of economic espionage, seems to have become interested in a new medicinal plant cultivated in the royal gardens by a gentleman named Damias de Goes from seeds brought back from Florida. When Nicot's cook wounded himself, Nicot is said to have asked Damias de Goes for tobacco. When the cook was cured, Nicot hastened to cultivate tobacco himself in his own garden and was soon besieged by sick people requesting pieces of the miracle plant. On 25 April 1560 he wrote to the Cardinal de Lorraine:

"I have obtained from a herb from the Indies marvelous proven properties against 'touch-me-not' and fistulas which doctors had given up as incurable, and bringing a rapid and singular cure to people who were in despair. As soon as it has produced seed I will send some to your gardener at Marmoûtier, and the plant itself inside a cask, with instructions as to how to replant it. ..."

Nobody now knows how Jean Nicot looked; nevertheless, he gave his name to the most famous of plants.

The cardinal was close to the queen. The queen suffered from severe migraines. She took tobacco in the form of snuff and her migraines faded away. Tobacco was launched in France and was baptized Nicotiana, Ambassador's Weed, Queen's Herb, Caterinaria. The first name was definitively adopted. The taste for tobacco turned toward madness.

In 1567 Jean Liébault, son-in-law of the famous printer Estienne, published a new edition of his father-in-law's posthumous work, *Agriculture et maison rustique* [*Agriculture and the Rustic House*], enlarged with several pages on tobacco: "Preeminent amongst medicinal plants by reason of its singular and almost divine virtues." The plant which he described was *Nicotiana rustica*, also known as "female Petum," and was the only one to possess the above-mentioned virtues: the "male Petum" completely lacked them. Liébault suggested changing the name Petum to Nicotiana, "after the lord who first sent it to France, in order to render to him the honor which he deserves from us for having enriched our country with such a singular plant." Numerous translations of *The Rustic House* throughout Europe would impose the name of Nicot on botanists, and Nicotiana eventually became nicotine.

The Rustic House was the first book to provide information on tobacco growing and to give details on its therapeutic applications. Already huge in the first edition, the list of afflictions which it could cure increased with vertiginous speed in

■

subsequent printings. Tobacco could cure everything. But this unrestrained enthusiasm quickly met with violent opposition.

1565. A year after the appearance of Liébault's rhapsody, the Italian Girolamo Benzoni published in Venice his *La Historia del Mondo Nuovo* [*History of the New World*]. He had spent fifteen years in America and had come back very critical of Spanish colonization and hostile to tobacco, pouring scorn on the supposed medicinal properties of the miraculous plant.

Another interpretation of Christopher Columbus's discovery of America in 1492. In the foreground, Indians bring him dried leaves which can only be tobacco. Behind them three men erect a cross. In the background, other Indians are running away. Engraving by Debry, 16th century.

"In *Espanola* [sic] [Haiti] and on the other islands, when doctors sought to care for a sick man, they went to the place where smoke was to be administered, and when he was completely intoxicated, this meant that the cure was almost ended. Returning to his senses, he recounted thousands of stories of how he had found himself in the meeting place of the gods and other visions of the same sort."

Benzoni considered this a repugnant form of drunkenness and insisted that "such a pestiferous and wicked poison can only be an invention of the devil," and he stigmatized "the stinging, fetid odor of this truly diabolical smoke. ..."

These detestations did not prevent tobacco from reaching Germany in the same year, 1565, when it was introduced by French Huguenots into Cologne and into England by Admiral Hawkins, the first British slave merchant. Thanks to another mariner, Walter Raleigh, it would rule at Queen Elizabeth's court. Then Benzoni's criticisms were swept away by the Faculties of Medicine. In 1571 tobacco was declared a medicament in Spain following the publication of the second part of the *Libro de las Cosas que Traen de las Indias* [*Book of Things which Concern the Indies*] by the famous botanist Nicolás Monardes, which boldly enlarged an already impressive list of ailments, illnesses, and wounds which could be treated by tobacco. Here we find it curing "venomous bites, chest problems of every sort, headaches, swellings, rheumatism, toothache, colds, congestions, stomachaches, constipation, kidney stones—indeed all afflictions caused by the cold." The work immediately enjoyed huge success.

Francisco Hernández de Toledo, physician to the Spanish king, prescribed certain treatments, including this one for asthma: "The dried, rolled-up leaves are inserted into a hollow stalk of reed or paper; one puts one end into the mouth or nostrils and, lighting the other, one draws in the smoke which arises, carefully pressing on the nostrils so that the vapors which descend into the chest make one expectorate marvelously and thus cure the asthma."

Tobacco was starting its grandiose career in Europe, and its detractors merely added to its renown. In 1572 the Parisian alchemist Jacques Gohory, otherwise an obscure character, succeeded in achieving notoriety with a treatise, *Instructions sur l'Herbe Petum, dite en France l'Herbe de la Reyne, ou Médicée* [*Instructions on the Herb Petum, Called in France "The Queen's Herb" or "Medicea"*].

In 1580 tobacco arrived in Russia, brought by the English; the Italians took it to Turkey in the same year. In 1590 it reached Japan thanks to the Portuguese. In 1595 the court of the Grand Mogul in India was contaminated. At the end of the century Persia, Morocco, Egypt, and the Philippines were infected in turn. The whole world had got to know tobacco but not the cigar.

MYTHS AND MAGIC

What was tobacco for the Indians, the first consumers? What was it in Europe in its earliest days? For the first it was sacred, for the second, magic. We have seen what virtues were attributed to it by doctors on the European side of the Atlantic, and for nearly two centuries. Across the ocean it had always been something else. In America tobacco preceded the creation of the world. It was an attribute of God. According to a Brazilian myth collected by the French missionary Martin de Nantes, it was God's representative on earth. Having decided to dwell in heaven, the All-Powerful sent tobacco in his place.

Engraving by Guillpino. Every class of woman smoked cigars in the Caribbean in the 19th century.

The Great Spirits of the Warao pantheon lived on tobacco smoke. They had unceasingly to be provided with it, otherwise the world would come to an end. Thus the sorcerers of the tribe were compelled to continuously smoke two-foot-long

Figure advertising an American tobacco retailer portrays an Indian woman holding cigars. Polychrome wood, North American Pacific coast, 1880.

Figure advertising an American tobacco retailer portrays an Indian holding dried tobacco leaves in his left hand and in his right a bundle of cigars with a strap around them. He is standing on a cart, which allowed the sign to be moved around more easily. Polychrome wood, North America, 1880.

(60–75 cm) cigars to which tacamahabo (*Pratium heptaphyllum*) gave an aromatic quality and which was mixed with incense granules.

In the beginning was the cigar, for the first Americans, from the Río Grande to the Grand Chaco, not forgetting the islands. In the north—it is unclear why— the pipe ruled, though tobacco was not considered less sacred. It played a key role in the life of hunters, whose trade was a priesthood. Likewise, the pipe would rule in Europe and the rest of the world until the end of the 18th century. Not the least strange aspect of the history of the cigar is the fact that for 300 years it was restricted to its original area, while its constituent material spread throughout the whole world.

It was the Mayas of present-day Mexico and Guatemala who celebrated tobacco to the highest degree. The smoking priest of the temple of the Palenque Cross, in the Chiapas, wearing a jaguar skin, his headdress a bird's head, and smoking a cigar, was one of the masterpieces of that magnificent civilization of the first millennium. It indicates the importance of the cigar. At the end of the 20th century, a thousand years after their ancestors abandoned the great cities, the Gods of the Four Winds and the Four Directions are still inveterate smokers, according to the Mayas of Yucatan. Shooting stars are the incandescent ash from their enormous cigars. Thunder is the sound of two great rocks which they strike together as a tinderbox, and lightning is the sparks which spurt from them. As for clouds, they are the smoke of the cigars of the God of Rain (from Libermann, in the *Encyclopédie du tabac*, Editions du Temps).

Tobacco, so long sacred in America and magical in Europe, in modern times is condemned as an agent of death, a survival of sensuous pleasures. "Syphilis," Malraux used to say, "begins with love." And as each of us is conscious of the fact that he will not live forever, longevity can only be relative. Sixteenth-century mariners and stevedores, Europe's first smokers, who regarded tobacco only as an object of pleasure, have triumphed over the learned and great men who sought to make it a remedy. Tobacco has no other use apart from giving pleasure. It has required more than two centuries to recognize this and two more to learn that it is harmful. To what point? Up until when?

Following pages: Ancient Mixtec ritual, fragment from the *Codex Vaticanus*, 16th century. The gods of ancient Mexico were ardent smokers.

A GREAT OMISSION

Amazingly, the cigar was left out of this great dispute on what was good or bad, beneficial or harmful. The eternal attribute of the American gods, a contemporary if not an agent of the creation of the world, a magic link between the Indians and

the Beyond, and their supreme pleasure, the cigar was nevertheless eclipsed by the pipe and even by snuff. The sumptuous fusees reproduced in the illustrations of André Thevet's *Cosmographie universelle* [*Universal Cosmography*] (1515), being smoked without exception by naked, athletic Indian men and women, remained unknown on the European side of the Atlantic. A trivial reason might be advanced: they wouldn't travel well. That is not enough to explain this ignorance: it would have been perfectly possible to make them with imported leaf from the 16th century, as was done in

André Thevet, a Cordelier monk from Angoulême, whose portrait, like so many others, is imaginary. It was really he who introduced tobacco into France.

the 18th. Why did such a simple idea take so long to mature? The first conquest of the cigar—unknown or disdained outside the West Indies, Brazil, and Grenada, which took in present-day Colombia and Venezuela—was a nation far removed from its original area: Burma. The entire population, men, women, and children, were gripped by a national passion as soon as tobacco was introduced. The Burmese even hit on the idea of piercing their earlobes, stretching them first no doubt, in order to slip their cigars into them and keep their hands free.

Attempts at introducing the cigar into Europe would for a long time come to nothing. In 1667, in Amsterdam, a Frenchman called Petit advertised in his shop at No. 56 Nyperstraat "rolls of tobacco, celebrated in the whole world and called cigars." As far as we know, he met with no success. In 1779, in Rome, a German tobacco manufacturer, Peter Wendler, obtained from Pope Pius VI the right to produce and market "tobacco sticks" (*bastoni di tabacco*) for a period of five years. It is not known that he made his fortune. In 1788 Hans Heinrich Schlottmann's cigar factory opened in Hamburg, a copy of the one in Seville where this German had undergone a long apprenticeship, without altering people's habits. In 1793, off Boulogne, the pirate Antoine Delpierre captured a Dutch vessel returning from Cuba, which provided fleeting happiness for the Frenchmen who tried out its cargo.

REVELATION

The manufacture of cigars really only started for France in 1816, and it was part of a European movement. Austria joined in two years later and called them "Virginians" in homage to the United States. One hundred and seventy million cigars were sold in 1848. The Germans and Dutch would quickly distinguish themselves. In the case of the first, the overwhelming development of cigar production, according to certain experts, resulted from a throwback which had inexplicably remained hidden. "The pleasure of smoking found a typically German expression in the cigar. In no other country has it been to this point such a symbol of the well-being and the boisterous feelings of the bourgeoisie." So writes Dr. Libermann in the *Encyclopédie du tabac*. Cigars would contribute to the formation of a powerful industry in Germany that reached its zenith in the "*Belle Époque*": in 1908 150,000 workers, men and women, produced 8.6 million cigars, not counting imports from Sumatra and Brazil. Cuba missed out cruelly in all this.

Imaginary smoker of an American peace pipe. Anonymous engraving.

Following pages: Walter Gay, *Women Cigar Makers in Seville*. Oil on canvas, United States.

Germany in 1788, France in 1816, Austria in 1818 … between the first two dates the United States got in on the game. In 1810 Pennsylvania began to roll its "stogies"—cigars about one foot (33 cm) long, rather like a double *panetela*, which were sold in packets of five and made with local tobacco. By the middle of the century the cigar had completely triumphed in the West. What had become of it meanwhile on the island of its origin?

A *marquista* portrayed in front of his plantation.

Unknown Cuba

Unsuspected at first, then incapable of being suspected of the best tobaccos, the homeland (like the Côte-du-Nord for the wine of Romanée-Conti or the Sauternes district for that of Château-Yquem), Cuba, astonishingly, was eclipsed for nearly a century by its neighbor Hispaniola (now shared between Haiti and the Dominican Republic). The imposture, or misunderstanding, seems to be complete bearing in mind that the word tobacco comes from Hispaniola. In his *Historia General y Natural de Las Indias* [*General and Natural History of the Indies*], Oviedo wrote:

"The chiefs and nobles had little highly polished and well made hollow sticks, about a palm long and the thickness of one's little finger, which branched into two little projecting tubes … thus they could put these in their nostrils, while they put burning herbs at the other, single end. … It is this instrument with two tubes and little sticks with which they receive the aforementioned perfume which is called 'Tabacco,' not the herb as some have hitherto supposed."

Thus the name of the container was taken for that of the contents; that of those kinds of nasal pipes for the name of the herb with which it was filled. Despite Oviedo, the error has persisted for three centuries. Its origin is attested by Hernández de Toledo in his *Cuatro Libros de Las Plantas y Animales en la Nueva España* [*Four Books of Plants and Animals in New Spain*]: "In the island of Española the name 'tabaco' is given to certain hollow reed shoots, about a hand and a half long, which were then filled with powdered charcoal, and some with tobacco, liquidambar (sweet gum), and other warm, sweet-smelling substances which, when

Goya, painter of genius and one of the glories of Spain, was the first to portray cigarette smokers, at the end of the 18th century.

Facing page: Three examples of the solemn style adopted by cigar manufacturers in the 19th century to promote their products.

lit at the end which has been filled, produce smoke at the other, which, when placed in the mouth, gently make one forget both the consciousness and all the fatigue of work."

The fortune of Hispaniola depended on chance rather than malice. The first Spanish colony in America, it was first to receive, circa 1537, seed of a Mexican

variety of *Nicotiana tabacum* originally from Yucatan, possessing an aroma and sweetness far superior to those of the *rustica* hitherto grown in the islands. Hispaniola was at once the pearl and the pivotal point of the Spanish empire of America, and *tabacum* would enhance its prestige. The mother country encouraged its production. Slaves were brought in from Africa to increase the ground area, the local Indians having already virtually disappeared, as much victims of European viruses as of their violence.

Cigar-box label ("*vista*") of the Don Pablo factory for Esquisitos tobacco. *Vista* of La Flor Cubana.

Quite unwittingly, Hispaniola usurped for nearly half a century a place which by divine right had belonged to its neighbor since the creation of the world. Cuba would have to wait for more than forty years for the seed which would do it justice, while its Spanish inhabitants, persuaded by the Indians that their island was bursting with gold, abandoned themselves to the latter obsession, using all their mental force and the power of their slaves in this quest. Once they had realized the vanity of their hopes of discovering Eldorado, they fell back on tobacco,

Though vigorously attacked in countless pamphlets, Marie-Antoinette was never accused of smoking cigars. Nevertheless her portrait was useful for publicity purposes.

Facing page: Léonard Defrance (Liège, 1735–1805), *Visit to the Tobacco Factory*, 1784. Oil on wood, 48 x 65 cm. Detail.

increasing their plantations of *Nicotiana rustica*, even though it was outclassed by *N. tabacum*, and for this reason were restricted to a home market or the satisfaction of the coarse sailors who passed by. From this time, notes the historian Ignacio José de Urrutia, the tobacco trade, though mediocre, was a prestigious affair in Havana, and the civil powers sought to regulate it, in other words, to restrain it.

The Spanish Oppression

The first prohibition dates from 1557. On 14 May of that year, the Havana municipal council forbade negroes, on pain of fifty lashes, to open or manage drink shops or any sale—even strolling sales—of wine or tobacco to the crew and passengers of the fleets which assembled at the harbor before crossing the Atlantic. This was done in order to reserve the trade more effectively to the white men from the mother country.

This racist arrangement inaugurated a long series of administrative acts which continued over nearly four centuries; almost all had the effect of victimizing the production and trade of a precious commodity, with the illusory goal of enriching a state that was prodigal by nature but ineffectual by vocation. Obsessed with total control, Spain controlled nothing, and her instructions remained a dead letter. English, French, and Dutch corsairs, pirates, and smugglers were completely at home in the West Indies. Over a period of twenty years Havana would be pillaged three times merely by the French, in 1536, in 1538—when the corsairs worked together with negroes in revolt—and in 1555.

Official Spanish tobacco literature would fill enormous libraries. Two samples of this output, dated 1781 and 1793.

On 16 September 1568 at the Escorial, Philip II, by royal decree, forbade all private trade in tobacco in Panama, on pain of a fine of fifty gold pesos plus the destruction of the incriminating tobacco. It was a question of destroying the commercial relations which had spontaneously grown up among Spain's various American possessions in order to divert them toward the mother country.

The attempt was of little consequence. According to Pezuda's *Dictionario*, from the end of the 16th century until the close of the 17th, smuggling outclassed official expeditions. But by how much remains the only question.

In 1606, Philip III gave way to a desperate measure, forbidding tobacco growing for ten years in the islands of Cuba, Margarita, and Puerto Rico, in the provinces of Venezuela, Cumaná, and New Andalusia. The text is worth quoting:

Certificate for 100 shares
in the Tobacco Products
Corporation of Virginia,
issued in January 1928 in
New York.

"According to letters from Don Luis Fajardo, my Captain-General of the Oceanic Fleet, and from my governors of the province of Cumaná and the island of Margarita, and from other competent people in my service, it appears that in divers places and ports of these islands of Barlovento there lurk numerous Dutch, English, and French rebel vessels in search of tobacco, which grows over there in abundance, being the principal crop of the natives; considering the quantity which they are able to seize, tobacco being greatly esteemed and sought after by the said nations, without my governors being able to stop it, and the prejudice which my rights are thus suffering … after deliberation and consultation with my Royal Council of the Indies, it appears to me appropriate to forbid the culture of tobacco in the said Isles for a period of ten years: thus the natives will be able to work in gold mines or transfer to other crops which will be more useful and advantageous for them and more profitable for the Crown."

This unheard-of interdiction, which could not be better enforced than the previous ones, was impossible to apply. Furthermore, Spain's rivals were easily able to procure seed in order to grow it in their own countries; in 1612 John Rolfe, the famous English husband of the Indian princess Pocahontas, introduced tobacco into Virginia.

Following pages: Léonard Defrance (Liège, 1735–1805), another version of *Visit to the Tobacco Factory*, 1784. Oil on wood, 48 x 65 cm. Detail.

CUBA RECOGNIZED. HOPES AND DISAPPOINTMENTS

Good sense prevailed again in 1614, two years before the end of the interdiction. On 20 October Philip III signed the first decree organizing the tobacco trade in Cuba, that of Cuba especially because it was already recognized as the best in the world. Not thirty years had elapsed since the introduction of *Nicotiana tabacum*, but the quality of its estates had prevailed; yet even so the Vuelta Abajo region would only come on stage a century and a half later. ... According to certain authors, England would pay its "weight in silver" for it; others say "its weight in gold." True, the English were crazy about tobacco. In 1615 alone they imported £200,000 worth from Trinidad and the Orinoco. At that time, the standing joke among the merchants of the Indies was: "We pay for English merchandise in smoke."

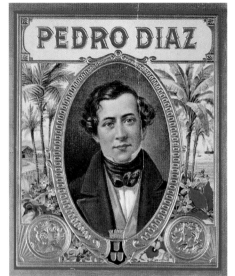

This serious-looking gentleman, set in an oval frame surrounded by palm groves and tobacco in flower, symbolizes the dignity associated with Havana tobacco at the beginning of the 19th century.

Spain stubbornly sought to proclaim an impossible monopoly. Madrid forbade its nationals to sell tobacco to foreigners under pain of death. The whole of the empire's production had to be routed through Seville, where the Casa de Contratación de Indias received a mandate in order to ensure worldwide distribution. Meanwhile smuggling prospered and clandestine plantations were being set up everywhere.

In his *Smoking Age*, published in 1617, the Englishman Bratwaith mentioned tobacco from Bermuda and Trinidad, and from Caracas and Barinas in Venezuela. All these tobaccos had escaped an unworkable monopoly. A very large proportion of so-called Bermudan tobacco came from Havana. The English corsairs of the archipelago, which never produced very much tobacco, waited there for vessels that had been loaded in Cuba and captured their cargoes. At the same time, the three nations mentioned by Philip III in his 1606 decree—England, France, and Holland—increased their overseas possessions in the West Indies and on the coasts of the two Americas. All three moved into Guiana at the same time: in 1623 the English seized San Cristóbal (later rebaptized Saint Kitts), and in 1624 they took Barbados; in 1632 the Dutch occupied Saint Eustache and Tobago; in 1635, the French appropriated Guadeloupe and Martinique. All three had scarcely landed before they started cultivating tobacco. At that time Madrid became fully aware of the value of Cuba. From 1632 on, tobacco from Havana imported into Spain was subject to customs duty, and its cultivation was declared a "gift of the crown."

During the 17th century Havana gradually became the capital of the production and dispatch of tobacco, not only toward Spain but the whole empire: Mexico, Costa Rica, the countries of the Pacific shore. "Nothing is more important than tobacco," they used to say in Cuba.

The first texts concerning important consignments from Havana date from 1626; they are secret denunciations accusing the governor, Cabrera, of having sent to the Canaries on his own account, without permission from Seville, a cargo of 200,000 pesos of tobacco. The Canary Islands, Spanish territory, were nonetheless the haunt of smugglers.

In the mid-17th century, with the encouragement of the governor, Don Juan de Salamanca, tobacco conquered the Santa Clara region. Under the name of Vuelta Arriba, or Remedios, this would become one of the island's two main centers. Why was it necessary to wait more than a century, until the 1770s, before the excellence of the estates of Vuelta Abajo situated around Pinar del Río in the west of Cuba, could be recognized? The entire world would be convinced of it in a few years. From the beginning of the 19th century the opinion would be quite simple: there is La Vuelta tobacco, and, far inferior, all the others.

Freedom of cultivation, regained in 1614, was mingled with absurd constraints. In 1717 Madrid had the first factory built in Cuba, at the same time as a monopoly,

The kings of France did not ignore tobacco either. With Richelieu, they were the first to tax it and impose a monopoly.

Lord Byron, surrounded by boxes of Havana cigars, was one of their first and most ardent propagandists; here he is perhaps meditating on his engagement on the side of the Greeks in the war of independence against the Turks.

identical to that of Spain, was established regarding strictly insular trade. This raised the planters' hackles, who immediately rebelled and took Havana. The crown representatives fled to Spain. The reaction was not slow in coming, and the rebellion was brutally repressed. A second revolt broke out four years later, in 1721, with the same outcome. A third met with the same result in 1723. The executed planters, who were only defending their own interests against an overly rapacious state, would one day be considered the first martyrs for Cuban independence.

George Nathaniel, 1st Marquis Curzon of Kedleston, viceroy of India (1898–1905), several times minister during World War I and the postwar period, was a great Havana cigar smoker.

Facing page: Plates from the *Encyclopédie* of Diderot and d'Alembert. "Rustic economy, making tobacco." France, 18th century.

Spain was not able to resist the temptation of out-and-out exploitation, for the fastest, not necessarily the largest, profit. In 1730 Madrid entrusted the monopoly to a syndicate of privileged traders, then ceded it in 1740 to the Royal Commercial Company of Havana, founded by Martín Arostegui under the pious patronage of Our Lady of the Rosary; twenty years later Madrid took it back again. Administrative delegations established in all centers of production negotiated the harvest with the deputies of the *vegueros*, who gradually organized themselves and standardized their cultivation, continuing to supply Seville.

Built in 1670 to manufacture snuff using the best foreign leaf, the Seville factory started to make cigars in 1720 with such success that a new establishment costing thirty million reales was constructed in 1757. It was in Seville that the cigar was to be invented that would conquer the world; "that is to say, according to Pedro Pérez, chairman of the Tabacalera—the first worldwide importer of Havanas and the oldest firm in the world as far as tobacco is concerned—a cylinder formed of a wrapper leaf, a binder leaf, and a filler." Seville dominated the manufacture and trade in the *puro* cigar which only Spain smoked seriously (even though tobacco growing was forbidden there, the only exception benefiting the Carthusian monks of Jerez, whose leaves were judged comparable to those of Cuba). The remainder of Europe lay in total ignorance of this new marvel. The West Indies and the "*terra firma*" lying near to America remained the kingdom of smokers. In his *Nouveau Voyage aux Îles de l'Amérique* [*New Journey to the Isles of America*], published in 1722, Father Labat wrote:

"The pipe is smoked very little in America. The Spanish, many French and English, almost all the negroes, and all our Indians smoke stubs, or 'cigales,' as the

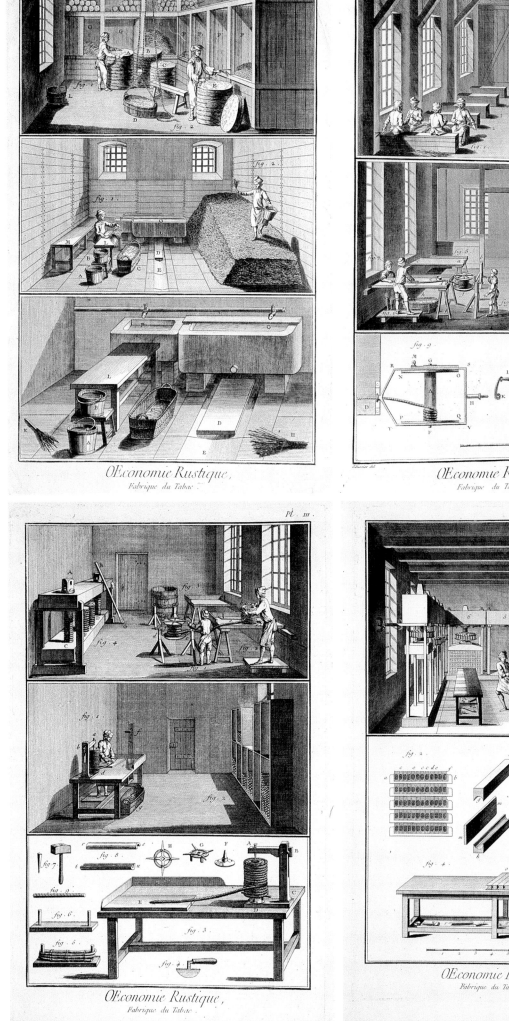

Pl. 1

OEconomie Rustique,
Fabrique du Tabac.

Pl. II

OEconomie Rustique,
Fabrique du Tabac.

Pl. III

OEconomie Rustique,
Fabrique du Tabac.

Pl. IV

OEconomie Rustique,
Fabrique du Tabac.

Cigar ring with portrait of President Fallières, 1906–12, Belgium. Juan López cigar ring with portrait of George V (major brand), ca. 1920, Cuba. José Gener cigar ring with portrait of Edward VII, Cuba. José Gener cigar ring with portrait of Queen Victoria, Cuba. José Gener cigar ring, with portrait of George V (major brand), ca. 1920, Cuba. Calixto López cigar ring (major brand), produced for the wedding of King Alfonso XIII of Spain and Victoria Eugenie, Cuba.

Spanish call them. The cigale, or tobacco stub, is a little cylinder six or seven inches long and five or six tenths of an inch in diameter, composed of tobacco leaves, twisted along their length, and wrapped in a piece of leaf which is called the 'robe' (wrapper leaf), which is neatly rolled around the first forming the middle of it and whose ends are secured by a thread. This part is held in the mouth, while the other is lighted."

This description was confirmed by an Englishman, J. Cockburn, in his *Journey over Land*, published in 1735. Recalling three friars whom he met in Nicaragua, he described their "seegars" in the following terms:

"These gentlemen gave us some Seegars to smoke. These are Leaves of Tobacco rolled up in Manner that they serve both for a Pipe and Tobacco itself ... they know no other way [of smoking] here, for there is no such Thing as a Tobacco-Pipe throughout New Spain [modern Mexico]. ..."

The earliest statistics go back to 1748. According to the Abbé Raynal, the anticlerical and anticolonialist author of the *Histoire philosophique et politique des établissements et du commerce des Européens dans les deux Indes* [*Philosophical and Political History of the Establishments and Trade of Europeans in the Two Indies*], between 1748 and 1753 Cuba exported an [annual] average of 800 tons of tobacco to Spain: an official average which did not take into account a huge amount of smuggling. What enthusiast would trouble to buy very dearly in Seville the tobacco that professional traffickers offered everywhere? Even the island itself, at this time, consumed more than 2,000 tons a year.

In 1761, the Factoría de Tabacos replaced the Royal Commerical Company of Havana in the delivery of crude products to the motherland. The Factoría, as its name shows, would henceforth operate in Cuba. Tobacco growing spread and moved. In 1762, when Spain was France's ally in the Seven Years' War, an English fleet seized Havana. The occupation was to last a year, until the Treaty of Paris was signed. The English and "American" troops (in fact the United States was only born in 1776) were conquered by the cigar. Havanas reached England in the tunics of red-coats and North America in those of the London colonial regiments. They were immediately a resounding success.

From 1789 to 1794 the official production of leaf touched the 3,000 ton mark. In 1804 the prices paid to planters corresponded to three categories: *suprema, mediana,* and *ínfima,* that is to say between 6.3, 4.7, and 2.5 piastres for an *arroba* of eleven and a half kilos (25 pounds), while the final price of a pound of cigars was six reales (or piastres); that of a pound of extra fine tobacco was 3.5 reales, that of a pound of ordinary tobacco—Seville *cucaracheros*—was 1.5 reales. At the end of the century the monopoly was bringing seventy million reales to Madrid.

Four varieties were cultivated from the 17th century, according to Rochefort's *Histoire naturelle des Antilles* [*Natural History of the West Indies*], published in 1658, and Dutertre's *Histoire générale des Antilles* [*General History of the West Indies*], between 1667 and 1671 (though Dutertre and Rochefort were perhaps one and the same). These four sorts of tobacco were the Grand (or Green) Petun, Harts-tongue Tobacco, Amazonian Tobacco, and Large-leaved Tobacco, which corresponded variously to the species *Nicotiana tabacum, N. brasiliensis, N. tabacum lancifolia havanensis, N. tabacum macrophylla,* and *N. tabacum havanensis macrophylla.*

Cigar-box label with portrait of Edward VII.

t the dawn of the 19th century, tobacco was no longer a remedy for anyone, merely a pleasure, "the only new voluptuousness" as Pierre Louÿs was to write a century later. A huge proportion of the human race was smoking pipes. Snuff-takers were becoming rarer; the French Revolution would deal a mortal blow to their aristocratic custom; even Napoleon was unable to maintain it single-handed. Tobacco chewers disappeared; they had never been numerous. The cigarette was unknown, except in Spain, where Goya had already painted it, but no one went to Spain any more and the Spaniards stayed at home. But for Spain, the only triumph which counts for real smokers was at hand.

After three hundred years of aberrant practices, people were beginning, just about everywhere, to ask themselves the key question: the best tobaccos

Page 49: The *marquista* Manuel López registered the Punch trademark in 1840 to facilitate his entry into the British market. It became and remains one of Havana's most famous brands.

Émile Fuchs, *Portrait of an Edwardian Gentleman*, 1901–10.

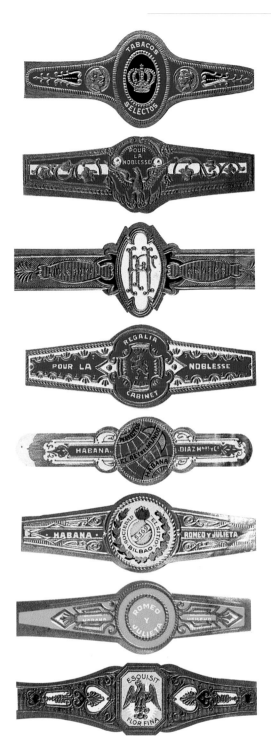

Top to bottom, modern cigar rings:
Tabacos selectos, with the image of the royal crown,
Germany. Pour la Noblesse, Belgium. Aigle royal,
with personal monogram HF, Antwerp, Belgium.
Pour la Noblesse, Belgium. Díaz, showing terrestrial
globe, Cuba. Romeo y Julieta, specially produced for
a paramilitary organization in Bilbao, Cuba.
Romeo y Julieta, Cuba. Esquisit Flor Fina, Belgium.
Facing page: Assortment of double *corona* cigar
boxes, the best on the market.

are Cuban—the Cubans smoke cigars—might Cuban cigars not be the very best there are?

"To every thing there is a season," we are told in Ecclesiastes. "A time to be born, and a time to die. ... A time to weep, and a time to laugh ...": the time of the cigar had arrived. Why was the evidence so late? Thousands of cigar lovers, rustic or refined, had passionately consumed tobacco in all its guises—as a chew, in poultices, in infusions, as smoke, as powder, even as a wash—and yet they had neglected the simplest way, the most natural method (together with chewing), the first known method, the best method according to general opinion, which must be worth something. What strange laziness ... ? The answer to this question would be too painful to human self-esteem.

It would be a brutal conversion, as if the converted, ashamed of their elders' blindness, wanted to blot out the three previous centuries.

Thus the 19th century began, in which progress became a cult. The glory of the cigar rose over the West. Illiterate Cuban peasants, Burmese with pierced ears, Spanish creators of *puro* cigars, pre-Columbian Indians who had long turned to dust, albeit dust tasting of tobacco, suddenly put on the radiant mantle of major precursors.

1810. The recording at Havana of the two first makes of cigar under the names of Bernardino Rencurrel and Cabanas y Carbajol. The year Marshal Soult entered Seville. There the soldiers of the Great Army would develop a taste for cigars. What cigars, which tobacco? The seas were blocked by the English fleets, Havana was cut off from the Spanish empire; at Trafalgar five years previously Admiral de Villeneuve had not taken enough care over his personal safety.

Seville had accumulated stocks. The vast storerooms of the Royal Manufactory, whose magnificent rows of buildings now house Andalusian students, were overflowing with leaves of La Vuelta tobacco. We may

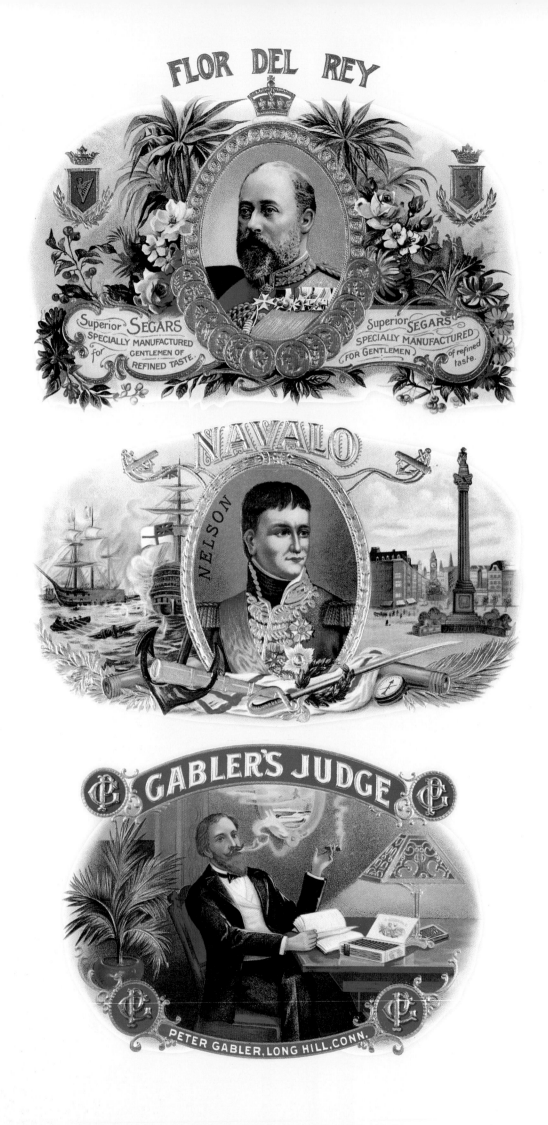

read in a document entitled *De la situación actual de la Real Factoría de Tabacos de la Habana en abril 1804* [*Concerning the Present Situation of the Royal Manufactory of Havana Tobaccos in April 1804*] that these reserves may have amounted to twelve million pounds of tobacco. Undoubtedly the French pillaged them, but for what motive? To teach the sensuous pleasure of Havana tobacco to people as far away as Moscow. (For their part, Wellington's English troops, dispatched against the ogre Napoleon in the peninsula, played a part in spreading, once they had returned home, the taste for the *puro* that they had first acquired in Havana in 1762.)

This sudden transport, as far as the distant limits of Europe, of an object which had been rejected for three hundred years, had something of fatality about it. It was as if a divine plan burst into the life of men, a plan which had long been in suspended animation—certainly divine, for this suspension was incomprehensible. An obscure yet brilliant design: at the same time as the soldiers of the empire and their British adversaries were becoming commercial travelers trading in very ancient novelty, things were on the move in Cuba.

CUBA AWAKES

Facing page: Other examples of vignettes that flatter both the manufacturer and the smoker. Edward VII was the incarnation of the British Empire, which was a world leader in his day. Nelson stood for British naval supremacy. The Americans of Connecticut, where tobacco plants were introduced in 1762, were satisfied with the image of a dignified-looking, cigar-smoking judge.

1817. The most famous snuff-taker in the world languished at Saint Helena, but thanks to him Europe had acquired a taste for the *puro*. His adversary, King Ferdinand VII of Spain, restored an absolute monarchy in Madrid but took modern measures in Cuba. He allowed himself to be inspired by a Cuban economist, Arango, and by his treasury secretary, Cangas, into abolishing the monopoly and the privileges of the Havana Manufactory, and allowing people to cultivate tobacco freely and to trade in tobacco. An instruction of 14 April 1817 organized the extension of plantations. He gave with one hand but took away with the other, replacing the ancient shackles by exorbitant taxes; It mattered little, things had been set in motion, the epic story of the Havana had begun. Scarcely had freedom been granted than a tax of thirty pesos per year and per worker "registered with the corporation of *tabaqueros*" was established on 25 November 1817.

The burden weighed so heavily on plantations that many of them foundered, until it was abolished. According to the *Memoria sobre la exportación del tabaco* [*Memoir on the Exportation of Tobacco*] by Bachiller and Morales (1836), they had to resort—as a stopgap!—to importing tobacco from the Dominican Republic and Virginia in order to satisfy Cuban domestic consumption. Exports did not suffer from this domestic crisis, as the new *marquistas* (owner-manufacturers) subordinated everything to them. These exports never stopped developing throughout the century, at least toward Europe, for relations with the United States were another story, despite the Ten Years' War and the War of Independence.

Cuban cigar-box label showing Buckingham Palace.

1827. The multiple taxes of 1817 were replaced by a single tax on the export of both leaf and manufactured tobacco. Energies which had for long been pent up exploded all at once. Supply multiplied the demand which had created it. The triumph of *puro* tobacco would know no limits other than those of production.

Shipping using the port of Havana increased from 1008 boats in 1816 to 1368 in 1820, then 1662 in 1836. The appearance of steam propulsion shortened the crossing time and multiplied the commercial exchanges, as well as the brands, factories, and plantations which supported them. In 1837 the island's tobacco production reached six thousand tons, having doubled since the start of the century.

Facing page: Upmann cigars, Havana, Cuba.

The number of cigar brands continued to increase. Mi Fama por el Orbe Vuelta appeared in 1830; Por Larranaga in 1834; Julián Rovera's El Figaro and Manuel López's Punch in 1840; Henry Upmann in 1844. The expansion was so powerful that around 1840 the *puro* cigar adopted the name of the Cuban capital and became the Havana. In 1844, as a defense against forgers, two of the greatest names in tobacco, Upmann and Partagas, registered their trademarks. In 1845 Don Jaime Partagas, who had founded his firm in 1827, installed his factory at No. 520, Calle de la Industria, at the junction of Old Havana and the new town. It is there still: the Real Fábrica de Tabacos Partagas is the showcase of the Havana in its very capital. A permanent flood of visitors from all over the world enlivens the Casa del Habano which has been set up on the ground floor.

Jaime Partagas owned vast plantations in the Pinar del Río region overlooking the *vegas* of Sandres and San Juan. An exceptional

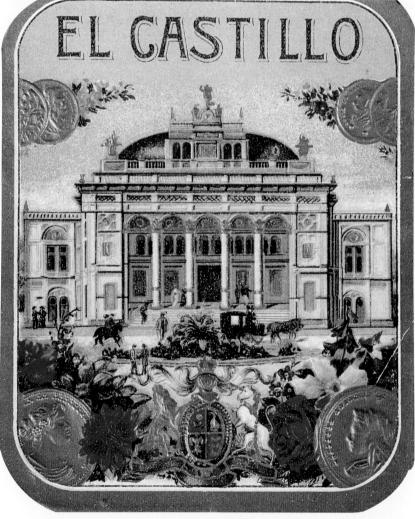

The cigar, according to its manufacturers, had always to be associated with symbols of
luxury and grandeur—big hotels, palaces, teams of horses, and elegance.

businessman, this irascible patrician launched his brand with impeccable mastery. "His reign lasted for 20 years," recounted Louis-Noël Barbulée in *L'Amateur du cigare*, "until 1864, when he was murdered during an argument which occurred at one of his *fincas* in the place called El Hato de la Cruz." His son José succeeded him but lacked his flair. He had to sell the business to José Bances, a powerful banker who was crazy about cigars, who retired in 1900 in favor of Ramon Cifuentes Llano and José Fernández. The latter soon gave up. The Cifuentes family would remain alone until Castro's revolution, controlling Partagas, Cifuentes, Ramon Allones, La Intimidad, and more than twenty other less important brands. Ramon Cifuentes went into exile in Florida, and, in association with General Cigars, launched a Partagas line in the Dominican Republic.

El Rey del Mundo and Sancho Panza, trademarks established by Emilio Ohmstedt, a wholesale trader of German origin, appeared in 1848. That same year the "Capitan general de la Isla de Cuba" imposed the official registration of all brands, which until then had been merely optional; their number leaped from 180 to 412. And the momentum was maintained. Romeo y Julieta, created by Inocencio Álvarez and Manin Garcia, appeared in 1850. In 1851 the Catalan José Gener founded Hoyo de Monterrey and started by launching "La Esception," with misspelled orthography, and offering magnificent cigars from the outset.

In the same year the Dutch trader Gustave Bock hit on the idea of putting bands around his cigars. Cigar bands immediately caught on. Thousands of famous persons—politicians, industrialists, artists, society figures—or those who thought they were, would, through their effigies and their renown, stand surety for *puros* which scarcely needed such a boost.

Top to bottom: Excelsior cigar ring. Romeo y Julieta cigar ring, personalized with the name of Juan Solans. Romeo y Julieta cigar ring, personalized with the name of Irezabal. Elegantes cigar ring. Rothschild Regalia cigar ring. Cabinets cigar ring. Cigar ring with female head in profile on a golden background, resembling a coin. Bock y Cia cigar ring with heraldic eagle.

Richard Dighton, *Portrait of Sir Richard Wallace*. Watercolor, ca. 1872.

Facing page: Hoyo de Monterrey cigars. Double *coronas* flavored with vanilla and honey,
considered one of the smoothest in this format.

The cigar is an attribute of the great and good in this world, and its image is worked out to conform with this idea. But the provenance cannot be ignored either. These vignettes showing Cuban landscapes forcibly make the point.

· NON PLUS ULTRA ·

SELECTION ESPECIAL

PLANTERS VERSUS STOCKBREEDERS

By 1831, approximately fifty Cuban cigar manufacturers were operating at Cayo Hueso (Key West) at the tip of Florida, opposite Havana. (A century earlier the Arnao brothers had settled there with sixteen workmen, but their venture came to nothing.) The number of these expatriates never stopped growing as the years went by and political conflicts tore the island apart. The emigration reached a climax at the time of the Ten Years' War (1868–78), set off by a revolt of the Oriente province.

The first departures of Cuban *tabaqueros* for Florida was the result of a dispute which would end only when the island achieved its independence and the republic was proclaimed; a classic case of a crisis in a new country between those who grazed animals and those who tilled the soil, the eternal tension between open space and enclosures, the wanderer and the settler. The question was spelled out by a local government circular, issued in the island on 15 September 1817:

"The organization of tobacco workers into *vegas* is one of those customs which it is right to continue taking into account; since their establishment, tobacco factories have always regarded this as an expression of a prerogative by virtue of which they have shared out and granted concessions of these *vegas*, for the exclusive growing of this plant. Thus a multitude of poor families have settled on the banks of the rivers, possessing official title to the land conceded directly or inherited. Their expulsion would run contrary to

Nineteenth-century plantation building showing the master's house and his workshops.

Exoticism would long characterize advertisements for
overseas tobaccos since they were colonial products.

every principle of justice and politics, and would cause the greatest damage to our essential agricultural and demographic objectives."

The great landowners opposed the settling of new planters by every means available and unceasingly tried to discourage existing ones, but history, even more than the interest of the mother country, ran against them. At Havana in 1837 Manuel de Soto y Quintana presented a memoir to the Economic Society of the Friends of the Country:

"It is evident that the hacienda system is incompatible with the progress of populations. It concentrates the riches of the lands involved in the hands of a few individuals, who reduce those riches to the acreage which they possess and who, even if they graze no cattle at all, would consider themselves betrayed if others acquired the tiniest piece of it. … The great estate owners are like the pine trees on their savannahs, which provide no shade for the traveler. From this springs the misery which afflicts a large proportion of the population, a lack of civilization and also of morality. I exclude from this brief analysis those few *hacendados* who are renowned for their probity and good deeds, who on the contrary help the *veguero* to settle in."

From the outset, the tobacco *vega* constituted a core of economic development which was inevitably in competition with the extensive pastoral activities of the haciendas: according to Article 27 of the Decree of 14 April 1817, prospective planters could expect a concession of a strip of land 120 yards wide measured from the banks of the river where they had decided to settle, not counting the land needed to provide their own food. The *veguero* was not only an agricultural competitor of the stockbreeder, the *vega* was inherently "a powerful force to undermine the hacienda system, for tobacco is par excellence an exportable product capable of generating incomparably large profits compared with those of the carefree stockbreeding of the great estate owners … something unprecedented in the economic history of America"—in

German cigar ring. Cigar ring, José Gener, Hoyo de Monterrey, with tobacco-plant motif. Cigar ring, Flor Fina, with palm-tree motif combined with coats of arms, Belgium. Cigar ring, Flor Fina, Princesas, Belgium. Cigar ring, Flor Fina, Inteligentes, Belgium. Cigar ring with coat of arms. Cigar ring, Flor Fina, with palm-tree motif combined with coats of arms, Belgium.

All the glories of humanity are employed in the service of the cigar. Here, great composers of the 19th century.

the words of the Cuban historian Le Riverend. A fair assessment considering the period, i.e., the second half of the 18th century and the first half of the 19th.

Furthermore, by "undermining the slave system" which prevailed in the haciendas and their sugar plantations, the *vega* permitted a rural bourgeoisie of small landholders to be formed, who were "freed from absentee landlords and destructive patterns of servitude" (Fernando Ortiz, *Contrapunteo cubano del tabaco y del azúcar* [*Cuban Counterpoint on Tobacco and Sugar*]). Tobacco was a business for free men.

Quite apart from differences of soil, climate, seed, and techniques, the black slaves who cultivated the American plantations during this period could not (perhaps because of their very slavery), in Cuban eyes, produce anything equivalent to the tobaccos of the *vegueros*, who always remained their own masters. Liberty transcended work.

TESTIMONIES

In 1842, the *Voyage pittoresque dans les deux Amériques, en Asie et en Afrique* [*Picturesque Journey into the two Americas, Asia, and Africa*] by two collaborators, Alcide d'Orbigny and Jean-Baptiste Eyriès, noted the fashion for cigars in these terms: "All the Creoles in the American colonies love smoking and offer small cigars when visiting. The cigar plays an important role in relations between the sexes: it is a sign of favor. For a woman, lighting a man's cigar by taking it in her mouth is an avowal."

The countess of Merlin also points out the role of women in the manufacture of cigars. The cigars smoked by planters, she noted at the same period, are "fashioned by their wives, their daughters, or their loved ones." The "stripper" or *despalilladora*—the girl who removes the midrib from the tobacco leaves—is as popular in Cuba as Carmen, the cigarette factory worker in Andalusia, notes

Ortiz in his *Contrapunteo*. But though they had always been entirely involved in tobacco processing in the country, women would for a long time be kept away from the Havana factories. Only at the end of the Ten Years' War, in 1878, would female workers be seen entering the cigar factory of La Africana.

In the middle of the century, a French traveler, Xavier Marmier, takes up the story told by the successive discoverers and writers of the West Indies:

"Part of the tobacco is processed on the spot by the individuals who cultivate it. The latter, who consume it, are not worried about the shape of the cigar, and these homespun productions are very cheap to produce; these cigars correspond to everyday bread compared with the fantasy-shaped loaves of the tables of the aristocracy."

"It is difficult to evaluate the quantities of tobacco thus treated. Only the factories could provide exact figures, and their total production averages 1,600 million cigars per year."

"There is not a single street in Havana which does not possess at least one factory; each of these factories employs 20, 30, or 40 workers or more, divided into teams, each devoted to a particular operation."

Jacques Offenbach, much-admired composer of *La Vie Parisienne* and *La Belle Hélène*, darling of the Second Empire and the "fête impériale," was unable to do without cigars.

Cuba also produced cigarettes, whose production would be mechanized from 1853, when Don Luis Susini imported a machine capable of producing 2,850,000 cigarettes a day.

Marmier's observations were published in Mexico in 1851 under the title *Cartas sobre la América* [*Letters concerning America*]. The following year Cuban tobacco production reached 20,000 tons, having tripled in fifteen years. Twelve years later, in 1863, Havana boasted no fewer than 516 factories employing 15,128 *tabaqueros*. To this number 36 manufactories should be added, plus the workshops of the Arsenal and the Bagne, where convicts worked, and the fortresses of La Cabana and La Carcel, where an average of 700 convicted soldiers manufactured cigars. But the overwhelming superiority of the "Havana cigar" would turn against the island.

■

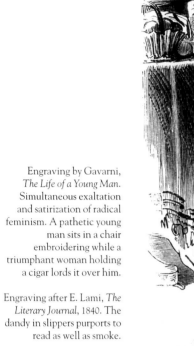

Engraving by Gavarni, *The Life of a Young Man*. Simultaneous exaltation and satirization of radical feminism. A pathetic young man sits in a chair embroidering while a triumphant woman holding a cigar lords it over him.

Engraving after E. Lami, *The Literary Journal*, 1840. The dandy in slippers purports to read as well as smoke.

Facing page: Paul Nadar, son of "Nadar" (Félix Tournachon), dressed up and photographed by his father. Caricature of a dandy smoking a cigar which, in fact, has not been lit.

with his fiery eloquence," recalls Gaspar Manuel Jorge Gallo in *El Tabaquero cubano* [*The Cuban tabaquero*]. The emigré *tabaqueros* "would officially contribute ten percent of their salary toward the revolution." "A sacred tithe offered at the altar of the fatherland," we read in Fernando Ortiz's *Contrapunteo*. The threat to Spain was so precise that Captain-General Salamanca multiplied his plots to "destroy the cigar-making centers of Cayo Hueso and Tampa in order to wipe out the rebel organization."

Mosaic depicting Jean-Louis Forain (1852–1931), who decorated the Café Riche on the Boulevard des Italiens, Paris, at the beginning of the 20th century.

The rostra of the Florida factories had their counterparts across the straits. They were really school-masters' desks rather than orators' platforms, where cigar makers were read to so as to occupy their minds as well as their hands. It is suggested that this educational practice had been inaugurated at Havana in the 1850s, at the Arsenal workshops, for the benefit of the "common rights" employed there, though the matter is unproven. It is known for a fact that the Reverend Manuel Delofeu, in 1864, set up permanent reading to workers in the cigar factory of Facundo Acosta, in the town of Bejucal. The idea had many years before been recommended by the Spanish traveler Salas y Quiroga. This novelty was influenced by a praiseworthy desire for social progress, doubtless influenced by the "public reading rooms" which were then very fashionable in the United States for popular education.

In 1865, the proletarian weekly *La Aurora* which the *tabaquero* Saturnino Martínez had founded at Havana, campaigned for reading, and the liberal Nicolás Azcarate—who would formulate the statutes of the tobacco-sorters' union at the end of the Ten Years' War—introduced it at the factory *El Figaro*. Partagas followed in his footsteps a few months later. On 15 January 1866 an editorial in the newspaper *El Siglo* recalled that in England Charles Dickens read his works to vast audiences of illiterate people who paid to listen. The Cuban cigar workers were not going to yield one step to the British illiterates. They accepted deductions from their salaries to pay those of their readers.

Down With Spain!

Two years later, in 1868, the first War of Independence against Spain broke out. The *tabaqueros* played a role of primary importance. Cuban political circles were divided between the reformists, partisans of a reorganization of relations with Spain, and separatists, partisans of independence. The strictness of a Madrid proconsul, General Tacón, who refused to apply the liberal Spanish constitution of 1836 in Cuba, strengthened the resolve of the second group. In 1865 the first group managed to bring about a meeting in Madrid of a committee which would study the Cuban situation and then sketch out the essential reforms: abolition of slavery, recasting of rights to land whose principles, which went back to the conquest, were unsustainable, tax reform, freedom of trade. ... The committee was still in Madrid when, on 12 February 1867, a Spanish decree added a new tax onto tariffs already considered absurd. The Creole bourgeoisie saw the measure as provocation and paused only a few months before acting.

On 10 October 1868, Carlos Manuel de Céspedes, a landowner and Grand Master of the masonic lodge Buena Fé, having freed and armed his slaves, proclaimed independence at Demajagua. The Yara revolution—from the name of his first victory over the Spanish—had begun.

Caricature of Edward VII by Sem, 1906.

In February 1869, the Armed Republic abolished slavery without delay or indemnity. In April the Guáimaro Assembly adopted a constitution which instituted a new single assembly and a president. Céspedes was elected.

Spain, having already lost all her mainland possessions in the Americas, would not cede Cuba. She reacted. The insurgents were divided. Terror ruled in Havana. José Martí, then aged 16, was condemned to six years' hard labor for a letter to a friend. Guerilla warfare replaced open war, the rebel chiefs were killed one after the other, but Spain was tiring. In 1876 the Spanish general Martínez Campos was sent to Cuba to restore peace, accomplished with the signing of the Treaty of Zanjón on 19 February 1878. From the insurgents' point of view, it was a confidence trick: slavery, though modified, was maintained, much to the Cuban patriots' indignation.

Jean Beraud, *Dinner at the Ambassadors' Restaurant*. Oil on wood, Paris. To the right, man with a cigar in his mouth, wearing a top hat; to the left, woman raising her little finger. Elegance is everywhere.

AFTER MADRID, WASHINGTON

The order for the start of the revolution was carried to Havana in a cigar that Fernando Figueredo, a *tabaquero* and general, had rolled at Cayo Hueso. This second war, even more than the first, developed under the banner of tobacco, whose flower with five points, white corolla, and red edging reminded Cuban poets and patriots of the national flag. Military operations began on 24 February in the Oriente region, where the Ten Years' War had already started. A coincidence? The revolt exploded after the Spanish General Weyler issued a decree reestablishing the old tobacco monopoly; Spain claimed to renounce eighty years of abolition and to reserve to herself the exclusive right of exports. These would fall from 15,000 tons to 6,000 tons within a year.

At the end of March, José Martí and Máximo Gómez, the military leader of the uprising, signed the Montecristi Manifesto. On 19 May at Dos Rios, Martí was killed in an engagement against the Spanish. Despite this loss and

Eternal womanhood reinforces the cigar's message.

CHAPTER III

20TH CENTURY: BIRTH OF A MYTH

1903 Romeo y Julieta was acquired by the millionaire Pepín Rodríguez, who immediately hit on the idea of buying the Capulet Hotel in Verona in order to promote his brand name more effectively. His eagerness only gained him a tobacco shop in the entrance hall.

In the footsteps of the Americans and Don Jaime Partagas, the great national cigar makers of this period integrated tobacco growing and manufacture: thus did Manuel López for Punch, José Gener for Hoyo de Monterrey, and Juan Francisco Rocha for La Gloria Cubana. The Hoyo de Monterrey *finca* at San Juan y Martínez, now the Hermano Saiz plantation, boasted 1350 hectares of cultivated tobacco. In 1928 two Americans took control of Rafael González.

Vignette in the national colors of Spain.

MONTECRISTO

The Montecristo brand, the most sold in the world, was created in 1935 by the brothers Benjamín and Félix Menéndez, who the following year acquired H. Upmann and, a little later, Por Larranaga, thus establishing themselves in the prewar period among the first rank of Havana cigar manufacturers, producing more than 25 million a year. They had gone into the tobacco business before the First World War, Félix as a buyer, Benjamín as a seller, in the Parra company, a trading firm, which they purchased in 1913 to create Menéndez and Company. Ten years later, the company changed its name to Menéndez y García with the arrival of an uncle, Alonso Menéndez, a retired businessman who came back from Tampa with a retired tobacco maker, José (known as Pepe) García. These additions encouraged them to enter manufacturing, restricting themselves at the start to the local market with the Particulares trademark; twelve years later they finally decided to attack the international market of most fantastic *puros*. These would become known as Montecristos.

Engraving by F. Giro on a square of golden yellow silk for El Dia. Manufacturer's publicity for its trademark. In the center, portrait of Dr. Don Bernardo de Yrigoyen.

Facing page: Montecristo No. 2 (*figurado*) cigars. *Torpedo* type and very powerful. Havana, Cuba.

Louis-Noël Barbulée has collected the reminiscences of Doña Dina Menéndez Bastiony, Benjamín's daughter, concerning the choice of this already fabulous name, which would become fabled a second time. It was one evening in Havana, in a café whose name has been forgotten, when the family had just decided to go on a trip to Mount Altube, when a bottle of Lacrima-Cristi was served, a wine from Mount Vesuvius, as everyone knows, and the two names of Monte Altube and Lacrima-Cristi were fused together as Montecristo. The mountain, the wine—and Alexander Dumas, no doubt—certainly brought them luck. It ought also to be pointed out that the historian of buccaneering in the 17th century, the Honfleur writer Oexmelin, mentions a place called Monte-Cristo, on the island of Hispaniola, next door to Cuba, in his *History of the Freebooters and Buccaneers Who Distinguished Themselves in the Indies*, first published in Dutch in 1678.

There were few other examples of such a fairy story in this period between two wars. The European "années folles" corresponded to less crazy years in Cuba. The fine period of the First World War, the dizzy rise of sugar prices, and the "dance of millions" had finished. Now crises and corruption went hand in hand. At the end of the 1930s the American Mafia ruled in Havana with Meyer Lansky and the blessing of the dictator Batista. *Puro* cigars, that symbol of luxury, escaped every misery.

Boris Artzybasheff, *The Busiest Man in Town*. Wood engraving, published in *Time*, New York, 1934–35.

Preceding pages: Closely hemmed in by his bodyguards, Fidel Castro, with a cigar in his mouth, prepares to sign a poster of himself for the admiring crowd.

The Second World War would leave good memories as far as tobacco was concerned. "We worked flat out for the Allies," recalls the oldest of the *chinchaleros*, small manufacturers who could be counted in hundreds in Cuba. "The difficulties began in 1945. Manufacturers laid off many employees."

Once the shock of peace had been absorbed, consumption was gathering pace again when, at the end of the 1950s, came the revolution. On 2 January 1959 Fidel Castro's insurgents entered Havana. Batista fled to the Dominican Republic. The damage would have been light if he had not been followed by a large number of cigar barons, owners of the biggest brands, including those of the Tabacalera Americana, reinforcing the vanquisher's conviction that the capitalists are incorrigible.

■

FIDEL CASTRO AND THE PURO CIGAR

Had the *marquistas* left Cuba? "The days of great brands have passed," proclaimed the *Máximo Líder* in 1960, to general astonishment. His closest companions may well have been astonished. However, the most popular of them, Ernesto "Che" Guevara, an Argentinian, is said at least to have urged him to stay his judgment. This intervention is less convincing when one considers that the following year, in his preface to Gaspar García's *Biografía del tabaco habano* [*Biography of Havana Tobacco*], he blew first hot then cold. "Sugar cane and coffee," he began, "originate in distant lands, brought here by the colonizer, then acclimatized, whereas tobacco is really ours." Unfortunately he continued as follows: "We are no longer the country of Havana tobacco but certainly that of Fidel Castro and the Cuban revolution." Havana tobacco, too famous, had to get back into line. "Its role is diminishing," he continued, "and we are not too concerned about this. Cuba in our view ought not to be just a simple producer of consumer goods intended to satisfy the whims of the few." These opinions could scarcely bring him to defend the great brands. They would change later, at least as far as Havana tobacco was concerned.

August Sander, *Portrait of a Banker*. Cologne, Germany, ca. 1932.

There was no stay of execution. The names, the boxes, the labels, the bands, the cigars which had established Cuba's glory for more than a century were suppressed. Thus, along with a hundred others, Henry Clay, La Corona, and Villar y Villar disappeared. The Menéndez family's H. Upmann factory, creator of the Montecristo, was renamed José Martí. There had been 960 kinds of cigar in Cuba, and this number was reduced to four, under the single name of Siboney, the patronymic of one of the patriots; four types manufactured under a state monopoly by a state company, Cubatabaco.

The consequences were immediate. Exports collapsed. Fortunately, far from remaining stubborn in his resolve, Castro displayed exceptional pragmatism. The land had formerly been nationalized; now the modest *vegueros* received back their properties—representing about 90 percent of tobacco growing—only the holdings of emigrés remained confiscated. Tobacco was saved. The cigar survived. How could production be started up again?

Emissaries set off for Geneva to consult Davidoff. This great expert and business-man recommended that traditional brands and production methods be reinstated. Che Guevara had not been listened to, but Davidoff was. Cubatabaco offered more than 300 types of cigar, with bands bearing famous brand names, no longer proscribed. While the band decorates the cigar, it scarcely makes it. Quality was hard put to catch up. In the world of cigar lovers, people repeated that it was not only the owners who had departed, but that the best professionals had followed them into exile. A series of bad harvests strengthened this pessimism. Criticism intensified: Havana tobacco was no longer what it once was, and the restored brands were frankly disappointing. Exports stagnated. Then the wind turned. The best professionals had not all left. They passed on their craft to pupils. The excellent harvest of 1964 and the consequent products convinced the most sceptical: Marxism and Havana tobacco were not incompatible. Lenin had demonstrated this in practice; why had it been forgotten?

White Cat cigar label, standard quality.

Facing page: Che Guevara, Cuba.

Following pages: Diplomaticos, a subsidiary trademark of Montecristo.
Groucho Marx in 1952. He never lit the cigars with
which he was photographed.

Dogs associated with cigars could only be the most fearsome ones, such as the mastiff and bulldog shown here.

Facing page: Aleksandr Mikhailovitch Gerasimov, *Portrait of the Artists Ivan Pavlov, Vasili Bakcheiev, Vitold Bialynitski-Biroulia, and Vasili Mishkov*. Oil on canvas, 1944.

Power and grandeur always go together with cigars;
here they are expressed in architectural form.

COHIBA

Thirty years later, no further proof was needed. Fidel Castro no longer mistrusted the notion of excellence. He had himself decided on and followed up the manufacture of a *puro* which would outclass all the others, which would be reserved for his friends, heads of state, and other people whom he was pleased to consider important. This cigar could not be one of the products of the old world, one of the ancient brands from the time when man exploited man. It had to be a symbol of the excellence of the new society, just as brands such as Henry Clay, Villar y Villar, and others had been that of vanquished capitalism. It would be good, too, if this new cigar bore a name linking it with the pre-Columbian Cuba of the Indians who taught the world to smoke cigars. Thus the name Cohiba was proposed, which the Arawak Taínos Indians, discovered to their cost by Christopher Columbus, had given to their tobacco and their cigars. It is said that this name, which symbolically wiped out four and a half centuries of colonial iniquity, was introduced at the suggestion of Celia Sánchez, standard-bearer of the Revolution and Fidel's lady companion, who proposed it to Eduardo Rivero, the key man in the process of selection and distinction which ended with the public launch of this outstanding *puro* cigar reserved for a long while for friends of the Revolution.

Sir Winston Churchill with his wife Clementine and their grandson Winston in front of 10 Downing Street, London.

For it was in 1962, three years after taking power, in the middle of the "revolutionary" crisis of Havana tobacco, before the Davidoff inspired reorganization and the 1964–65 harvest which ended the problems, that the adventure began.

Eduardo Rivero was twenty years old. He had been rolling cigars for seven years. He was the friend of Bienvenido Pérez Salazar, called "Chicho," head of Fidel Castro's bodyguard. Rivero put together a cigar different from the others which he tried out on his friend. "One day," he recounted, "at the very start of the revolutionary government, Fidel, closely followed by Chicho, smelled one of my cigars and showed an interest in its aroma. Chicho told him my story. … That is how I became the exclusive supplier to the commander in chief and his escort."

■

In 1963 Fidel decided to set up the "Plan Especial de Tabaquería" and to open a factory dedicated to this supreme cigar, whose output he would test himself.

"Fidel has an extraordinarily sensitive palate," affirmed Eduardo Rivero. Two hundred prostitutes were given a new job in the new factory, installed in the abandoned palace of the marchioness of Pinar del Río, in the beautiful Cubanacán

Upmann and Partagas, two of the greatest and oldest names in Havana. The Partagas building, main showcase for the *puro* in Havana in the late 1990s.

quarter, capital of the Vuelta Abajo ("chance has no place in the government of human affairs," as Bossuet remarked). This name of Pinar del Río had been chosen by Leopoldo González Carbajol, a descendant of the Cabanas family, one of the oldest tobacco dynasties—the Carbajol brand dated from 1810. The new factory bore the name El Laguito, and Eduardo Rivero became the manager. He was not content with personally choosing the finest leaf from the best *vegas* of La Vuelta and keeping the closest possible eye on every single stage in the process of producing his marvelous work, including the triple tobacco fermentation process, about which he did not make a great fuss (unlike others, for whom triple fermentation was considered the essential secret of the quality of Cohiba). "Triple fermentation," Rivero used to say, "is part of the normal process of creating a quality cigar." In 1967 he started up a plantation reserved for his factory "to guarantee production." But the marvel still had no name. He had to find one. It was in 1968 that Celia Sánchez …

In 1968, too, the liquidation of capitalism came to an end, with the exception, once again, of agriculture. Brigades of patriots were given the task of blotting out all trace of it, starting in Havana with the brand names displayed on the façades of buildings. Those same brands whose names had been revived for the Cubatabaco factories at the time of the "great return to the past" which served to correct their disastrous suppression in favor of four types of Siboney cigar. Although the trademark names were printed on cigar bands, the authorities no longer wanted to see them on signs.

The zeal of the revolutionary brigades was not implacable. In 1995 the magazine L'Amateur du cigare sought out traces of those signs in Havana, and the researcher did not come back empty-handed. One can still see on the façade of No. 2 Padre Valera Street, incised in stone, the glorious name Romeo y Julieta, with the figure 1903 above it, the year the factory was built, on the former site of the capital's bull-ring. Some windows open into emptiness, a part of the building having collapsed in 1993, others light inhabited rooms, and charming females emerge, among the drying wash and the bicycles, onto balconies enlivened by Caribbean wrought-ironwork. The names La Corona, Por Larranaga, La Excepción, Ramón Allones, and about ten more, could be discerned. At No. 864 Belascoain Street, El Crédito, founded in 1898 by Calixto Mauri with seven employees, rising to 800 in 1914, now harbors the printing works of the central committee of the Cuban Communist Party. On the corner of Máximo Gómez Street and Bélgica Avenue, La Meridiana, built in a most luxurious style by Pedro Muria in 1860, has become the ministry of foreign trade. As for Calixto López, in Zulueta Street, dating from 1850, it has not abandoned its calling: Habanos S.A. has installed its offices there.

To finish with Cohiba, El Laguito in the late 1990s employs 250 people, and for Cuban officials, who can scarcely say anything else, bearing in mind its origin, the Cohiba is the best cigar in the world. Impartial cigar lovers heatedly discuss the matter.

Cohiba cigar.

Jiggs, character from the comic strip by George McManus. Caricature of the elegant, idle American.

Havana and the Revolution

Fidel Castro, who eventually stopped smoking, proved himself over the years to have been such a great smoker that he could surely find little wrong with the cigar itself, symbol of Cuban excellence. It was the *marquista* capitalists who aroused his wrath. The cigar on the contrary has benefited from his revolution. Antonio Núñez Jiménez, Doctor of Philosophy, once "Che's" aide-de-camp, former ambassador and vice-minister of culture, author of a *Study on the Discovery of Tobacco* and of a *Book of Tobacco* published in Mexico in 1994, and now director of the Foundation for Nature and Humanity, a great smoker of peasant culebra cigars (a three-in-one twisted cigar), has precisely stated the role of the cigar as follows: "During the first years of the Revolution we scarcely ever slept. Between combats the stimulating effects of the cigar helped us to keep awake." Che Guevara, he recalled, smoked his first cigar in the Santiago bush. After the victory came the agrarian reform; Antonio Núñez Jiménez was one of the organizers and was not able to sleep either. "We did not even have time to eat, and cigars allowed us to overcome our hunger all day long."

Guevara, who had suffered from asthma since the age of two, began to smoke cigars in the Sierra Maestra, copying his companions, in order to keep the mosquitos at bay. He used to cut his cigars in three pieces, placing them in a pipe; then he gave up the pipe and smoked them whole. He used to smoke three or four Partagas or H. Upmanns a day, drawing on them until he burned his lips, for he detested waste. He smoked them in stages, letting them go out after a few puffs, relighting them later. Before he left for the Congo, where he tried to create a second "Vietnam" in 1965—he dreamed of starting a whole series of them in order to bleed capitalism to death—Antonio Núñez Jiménez worried about Che's asthma and begged him for a long time to listen to the doctors (Guevara was one himself) and to give up smoking. "I would like to be allowed to smoke one *tabaco* a day," he conceded in the end. And the next day he sported a cigar three feet long, which he had rolled himself, and which bore his name. His biographer, Jean Cormier, relates that in 1967, when he was in Bolivia, Régis Debray brought him two boxes of Churchill cigars. He shared them with his guerillas.

Following pages: Magritte, *L'Exception*, 1963. Oil on canvas, 33 x 41 cm, Belgium. Half cigar, half fish, this strange creature does not express happiness.

Chapter IV

Tobacco Growing and Manufacture

In Havana

At the end of the 20th century, the cigar is almost absent from Havana. There are few smokers and they are all old. Without smoking themselves, young people manage the key tourist spots of the old town and the pavements outside hotels, offering fake *puros* at a third, a quarter, even a fifth of the price of the genuine famous brands from which they have been copied—La Corona, Partagas, Cohiba. On the other hand, the few factories open to the public are invaded by foreigners who come out of their shops with bags full of marvelous things. The Casa del Habano, owned by the corporation Cabanacán S.A., on the ground floor of the Partagas factory, the *puro*'s main showcase in Cuba and never empty, sells an average of 2,000 cigars per day, 80 boxes in the classic format of 25 each—a figure to be compared with the output of the actual factory, subject to UNETA (Union of Tobacco Enterprises): the latter produces 22,000 per day or 4,200,000 per year (figures from 1995 and intended to be maintained thereafter), that is to say, around 7 percent of the entire island's total export production.

In the country, in the Vuelta, smokers are more numerous, with a *culebra* [pigtail] in their mouths. Cuban men, but not Cuban women—a curious infringement of equality—have the right to four Havanas a month, *puros* for domestic consumption, whose purchase is noted down in their ration books. Even if they are not smokers, they buy them conscientiously, in order to pay for the tiny luxuries that make their lives more tolerable.

Cigar-box label for El Tolna cigars.

DISASTER AND SOLIDARITY

Havana tobacco has experienced disastrous years. The disappearance of the Soviet Union, mainstay of the Cuban economy, plunged the island into a terrible crisis. Suddenly everything was lacking. The "special period" of general rationing, together with the individual ration book—the *libreta*—began. On the tobacco plantations, deprived of fertilizers and chemical treatments, a type of mildew known as *Mohul azul* (blue mold fungus) destroyed 80 percent of the 1990–91 crop, a loss impossible to make good. The harvests in 1991–92, 1992–93, and 1993–94 were worse still. *Mohul azul* was overcome, but violent rainstorms ravaged the plantations. The dearth of production methods had now come to an end. The great importers and distributors of Havanas, the Spanish in the lead, followed then by the French, have taken the place of Russia in an understandable movement of commercial solidarity.

Adriano Martínez, commercial director of Habanos S.A., which succeeded Cubatabaco in December 1994, resumed his activities for *L'Amateur du cigare* in 1995: "The people from the Tabacalera (Spain), like those of SEITA (France), granted us credits, the first much more important than the second (Spain, who discovered the cigar and fixed the norms for the manufacture of the *puro* is its largest consumer in the world). Thanks to this, we are in a position to guarantee them a supply of Havanas and of the raw tobacco which they need. What is more, they help us to increase our productivity and thus to sell more to other customers. All our importers, all our foreign distributors played a part in financing the 1994 and 1995 harvests."

With the financial question settled and pests eliminated, there remained the uncontrollable temper of the heavens. In February 1995 a band of cold and rain— rain is tobacco's main enemy—destroyed one-third of a harvest that had promised to be superb. The *tabaqueros* planted out their devastated plantations a second time by drawing on their reserve seedbeds. Heaven rewarded them. Until the end of March the cold and rain gave way to humidity and coolness, ideal conditions. Soon the tobacco was splendid and the quality of the leaf exceptional. The harvest surpassed the 33,000 ton mark. Habanos S.A. adjusted its forecast deliveries to the international market to 70 million cigars; these had not exceeded 55 million in

Facing page: Havana is worth the journey, were it only for this sight alone.

Pricked-out Corojo tobacco plants, intended for quality wrapper leaf, are protected from
direct sunlight under huge, fine cotton-mesh cloths known as *tapados* (shown above); these ensure the
correct temperature and humidity for their leaves to mature to perfection (shown below).

equipment being a plank and a *chavette*, a very sharp crescent-shaped blade used to cut the binding and wrapper leaves. To the untutored eye, the cigar rollers' skill and economy of movement are nothing short of miraculous. It is they who turn the cigar into that perfect object whose very contemplation already engenders a feeling of well-being in the cigar lover. (The Cubans say that ten years are needed to make a good *torcedor*—ten years, and genius.) Once the cigar has left the hands of the *torcedor*—or *torcedora*, for women had being infiltrating the profession in force since the revolution—the banders, more often women than men, place the cigar bands

The drying process taking place in the "tobacco house" of José Manuel Sisto at Viñales. Cuba, 1996.

on the cigars with fairylike fingers. Then those responsible for storing the cigars place them in large pieces of furniture like colossal cupboards, where the cigars gently recover from the violence they have suffered in order to achieve perfection (the tobacco has been stretched, twisted, compressed, and must now relax and lose the surplus humidity which it was necessary to add to allow it to take the necessary shape without breaking). Then the packers cajole the cigars into their cedarwood boxes, with their bands properly lined up and each paper medallion facing upward. Finally, the impassive labelers stick on the boxes those green tickets of authenticity which throughout the world inspire the most violent feelings of respect, envy, covetousness, and of frustration when the box is simply waved under one's nose, whether open or closed. All the workers' actions, however rapid (as some of them, such as stripping have to be), seem imbued with a marvelous gentleness. For there could be no cigars without caresses.

Thermometer used to measure the temperature within the mound of tobacco leaves.

ATMOSPHERE

Facing page:
Bundles of tobacco,
Cuba.

Today Pinar del Río scarcely seems to have changed since the colonial period. It is a charmingly dilapidated checkerboard of low buildings provided with painted colonnades, simple or elaborate, and displaying every imaginary architectural order, starting with the Doric, Ionic, and Corinthian. Verandas are essential, and the rich style of the numerous iron balconies recalls the *mudéjar* style of Seville. Quite close to the town center, the Francisco Donatien cigar factory employs thirty workers—mostly female, many of whom are very jolly, some very gracious, and some very engaging—behind its sky-blue columns. They make cigars reserved for home consumption: Cazador, Nacional, Petit Cetros, Brevas. Furthermore, a fine shop where tourists in ecstasy elbow each other offers fine cigars by the great export brands. An unceasing convoy of dusty buses—Cuba wisely saves on tarmac, and rain is quickly dried by the sun—renews this clientele from dawn till dusk.

All around the famous villages of San Juan and San Luis, the countryside undulates gently as far as Consolación del Sur, eastern frontier of La Vuelta. These

undulations, cut through by rivers, are not pronounced enough to prevent the area from forming a plain, limited to the north, toward Viñales, by the abrupt escarpments of the Sierra de Rosario, impressive bluffs of Upper Jurassic limestone, swathed in jungle like a royal robe. It is one of those plains that has been divided up by the old self-sufficient peasant estates, an apparently anarchical division into irregular plots for tobacco, maize, pasture, and vegetables. Almost ripe tobacco plants stand side by side with plants just pricked out, a juxtaposition explained by the fact that the season lasts six months and tobacco grows fully in three. Tethered in the meadows, emaciated cows try not to get thinner still by cropping the rough grass which poorly covers their pasture areas, circles about 45 yards (40 m) across, though rather irregular because of the hilly terrain. Parasitic birds watch over this cattle, one to one, each beast possessing its bird.

Cigar-leaf stripper at Viñales.

Facing page: Cigar rollers in the Partagas factory in the heart of Havana.

From the Jasmine Hotel which overlooks Viñales, whose surrounding land—Vega 14—is not the best but is certainly the most beautiful, the whole land goes black when night falls. At first, not a single light betrays the presence of humans. Ponds and lengths of stream, glimpsed between two meanders, are the only bright patches in this most celebrated part of Cuba. Then the lights of a former age begin to appear, old-fashioned fires, candles, and lanterns. The silence is broken only by lowing, bleating, occasional braying. The 20th century makes its presence felt, very occasionally, by the noise of a motor: the muffled gurgling of the big five- or six-liter engines that American cars boasted between the 1930s and the 1950s, which survive here in great numbers, kept going by fanatical mechanics, and apparently lasting forever.

This countryside, bristling with palm trees, including the "paunched" type whose name indicates its shape and the royal palm, a gray rocket whose green topknot ends in a lightning conductor, is littered with "tobacco houses"—the

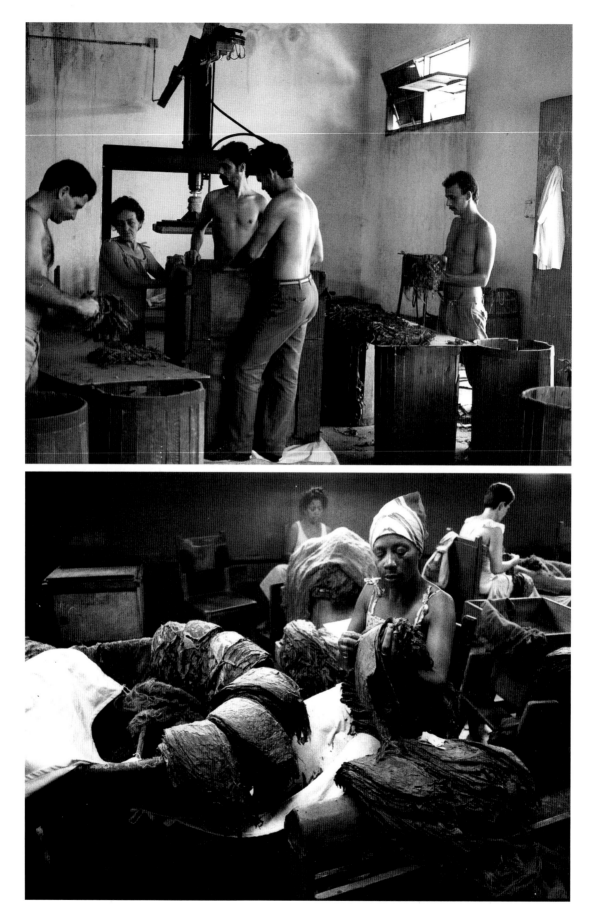

Above: Stripping tobacco leaves at Viñales.
Below: Sorting leaves by size at the H. Upmann factory, Havana.
Facing page: Cigar roller's bench with the molds in which cigars are compressed before the binder
and wrapper leaf are added.

Above: Sorting cigars by color.
Below: Sorting cigars into bundles.
Facing page: Calibration and quality control.

Above: Putting cigars into boxes.
Below: Attaching the cigar-box labels, 1996.
Facing page: Partagas factory. Havana, 1996.

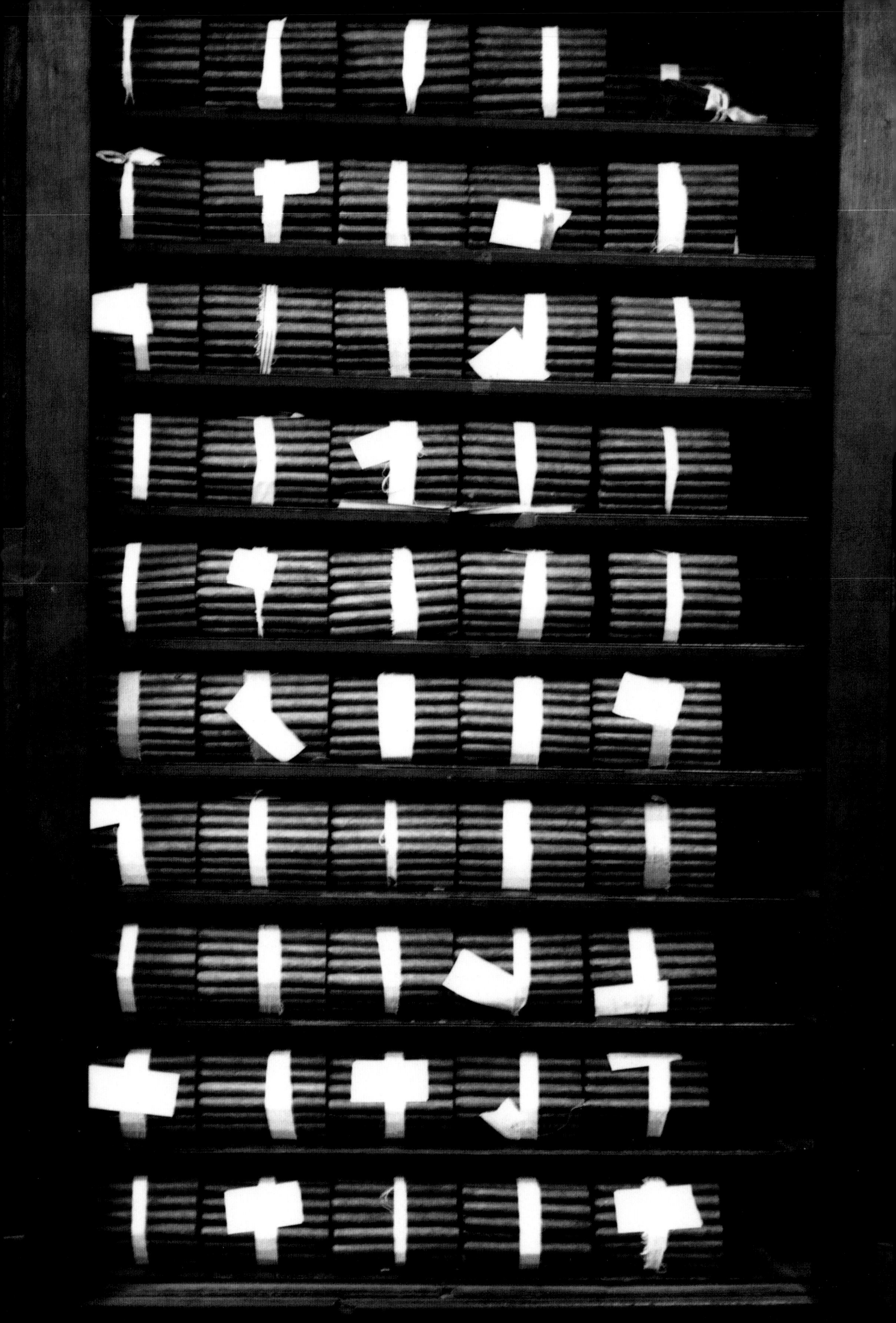

drying-houses of the *vegueros*—closely resembling huge gray tents, for their double roof slopes of dried palms reach right down to the ground. There, in the silence and the drafts which cleverly flow through them thanks to sets of windows with shutters arranged in the end walls, lines of leaves astride their perches dry and breathe in the shade without rustling at all. Toward San Juan the "snowfields" become more common, huge cotton sheets placed 6 feet (2 m) above the ground on a forest of supports to shelter the tobacco from insects, temper the strength of the sun, and

Reader in action in a cigar factory.

keep in the precious humidity. Underneath them, plants 4 feet (1.5 m) high are all attached by cotton threads to their protective veils. Thus they cannot be flattened by the wind and, above all, their leaves enjoy optimum exposure to the light. The peasants who have worked these red lands since time immemorial are masters of tobacco. They work by hand, and their carts are pulled by oxen. Their houses—the *bohíos*—often covered with palm fronds, measure about 30 (10 m) by 18 to 20 feet (5–6 m) and are shaded by lemon trees, orange trees, grapefruit trees. Hens scratch at the ground all around. In the evening, the peasants sit in rocking-chairs on the verandas and take a break from tobacco by smoking cigars. A bucolic lifestyle

Facing page: Maturing cupboard where cigars lose the excess humidity added during the manufacturing process.

recalling Virgil's *Georgics*. ... Everything is ancestral, Virgilian, in the growing of the best tobacco in the world and the *puros* which are made from them. This results no doubt from circumstances. The American embargo is primarily responsible for this anachronistic lifestyle which the visitor from so-called developed countries finds so charming. As for the *vegueros*, they would certainly love to have tractors and machines; who could blame them? Would the *puro* benefit from this? It is an open question. Cigar lovers who argue about such things would do so less bitterly if they were not aware, or had at least an inkling, albeit of the most fleeting and astonishing kind, that they were living the last moments of a miraculous "suspension" of time—few miracles can ever have been so ambiguous—over Cuba. In the fragile world of the cigar, the Cuban revolution has for the past thirty years practiced an ideal form of conservatism.

Peerless presentation of a box of Lusitanias, the Partagas double *coronas*, among the best available.

Facing page: *Catador* (cigar taster) at work. His opinion is indispensable; consistency of quality depends on it.

INDONESIA

The production of tobacco in southeast Asia was formerly concentrated in the Philippines around Manila and in the Cagayan valley. Now it is located in Sumatra and Java.

SUMATRA

The Medan region, in the north, produces tobaccos intended for European, machine-rolled cigars.

JAVA

By far the more interesting of the two islands. To the east, in the province of Bekasi (Jember), Bekasi wrapper leaf is cultivated in the open air and TBN wrapper leaf under mesh cloth. Sent to manufacturers in the Caribbean, they complement deliveries from central Africa and Connecticut.

TWO VARIETIES:

Mexican Sumatra (light tobacco)
Mexican wrapper and binder leaf

MEXICO

HONDURAS
San Pedro Sula

TEGUCIGALPA
(Danli)

SECONDARY TOBACCO-PRODUCING REGIONS

Brazil produces filler leaf in the Bahia region.

Ecuador produces wrapper leaf of Connecticut type, which supplies manufacturers in the Dominican Republic.

Honduras has two production centers. The main one is in the north, in the Sula valley (San Pedro Sula), the other is in the south, around Danli and Tegucigalpa. Certain cigars now available in France are made there. The tobacco is light with a rather woody aroma.

Mexico produces two interesting varieties. Mexican Sumatra produces wrapper and binder leaf (on the light side) which are exported to the Dominican Republic; Mexican tobacco is black, used for the wrappers and filler of American cigars.

ECUADOR

Connecticut wrapper leaf

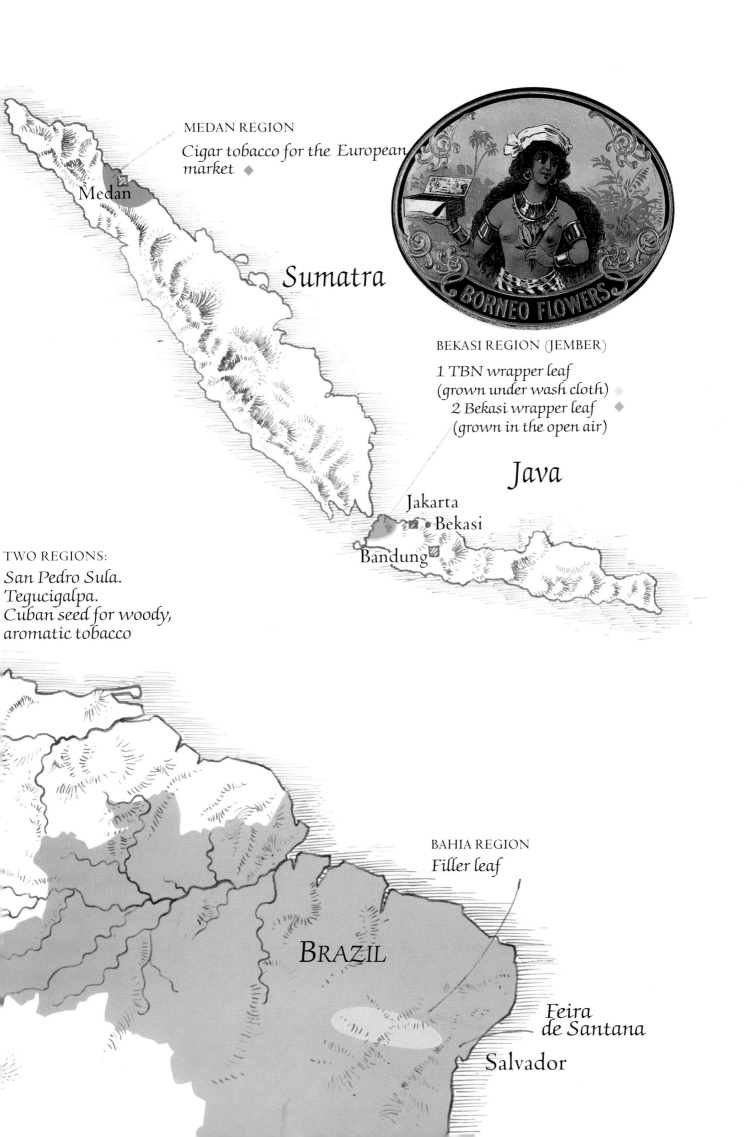

MEDAN REGION

Cigar tobacco for the European market ◆

Medan

Sumatra

BEKASI REGION (JEMBER)

*1 TBN wrapper leaf
(grown under wash cloth)* ◈
2 Bekasi wrapper leaf ◆
(grown in the open air)

Java

Jakarta
Bekasi
Bandung

BORNEO FLOWERS

TWO REGIONS:

*San Pedro Sula.
Tegucigalpa.
Cuban seed for woody,
aromatic tobacco*

BAHIA REGION
Filler leaf

BRAZIL

Feira
de Santana

Salvador

*C*olor used to be an essential criterion in the choice of a cigar. Some smokers of *colorados* would never have considered choosing a *maduro* or vice versa. The brand came in second place when making one's choice. Today the myth is dying out because color affects only the wrapper leaf, i.e., three to four percent of the product; it does not really have a significant effect on the taste of the cigar. Color remains, notwithstanding, one of the elements allowing families of cigars with significant differences to be distinguished.

CLARISIMO OR GREEN: These are also called "candles" from the Spanish *candela*. The greenish color of the wrapper leaf is determined by rapid drying before the tobacco has cured. These are generally cigars made for the American market, with an inconsistent flavor and insipid taste. In particular cases the color of the wrapper leaf can influence the character of the cigar.

DOBLE CLARO, CLARO-CLARO, OR BLOND: A very light gold color tending toward pale yellow, this shade of brown is also obtained by picking the leaf before it is fully ripe and by an accelerated drying process.

CLARO OR WILD HAVANA: A brown tobacco, on the pale side, the leaf is often picked before the *maduros*. This light-colored leaf covers many cigars, which are classified as being among the lightest.

COLORADO CLARO OR LIGHT BROWN: These are picked later and subject to longer fermentation, which explains the appearance of the leaf, at the start of the "brown" series, bringing together cigars with more consistent body.

COLORADO OR MEDIUM BROWN: More developed maturing of the leaf and longer fermentation provide wrapper leaf for the more highly regarded cigars.

MADURO COLORADO OR BROWN: First of the dark cigars, its leaves are chosen from the top of the plant, which have received more sunlight; a longer curing process produces a type which is often high flavored. The Montecristo No. 3 is an example.

MADURO: With still more exposure and longer fermentation, or the use of Connecticut type tobacco, these are the cigars which in theory are only suitable for experienced smokers, for they are extremely full-bodied. In practice, certain Honduran and Dominican *maduros* are of reasonable strength.

OSCURO: The highest rung on the ladder and very widespread in the 19th century, this almost black color is nowadays quite rarely seen. The Onyx brand, distributed on the American market, includes a certain number.

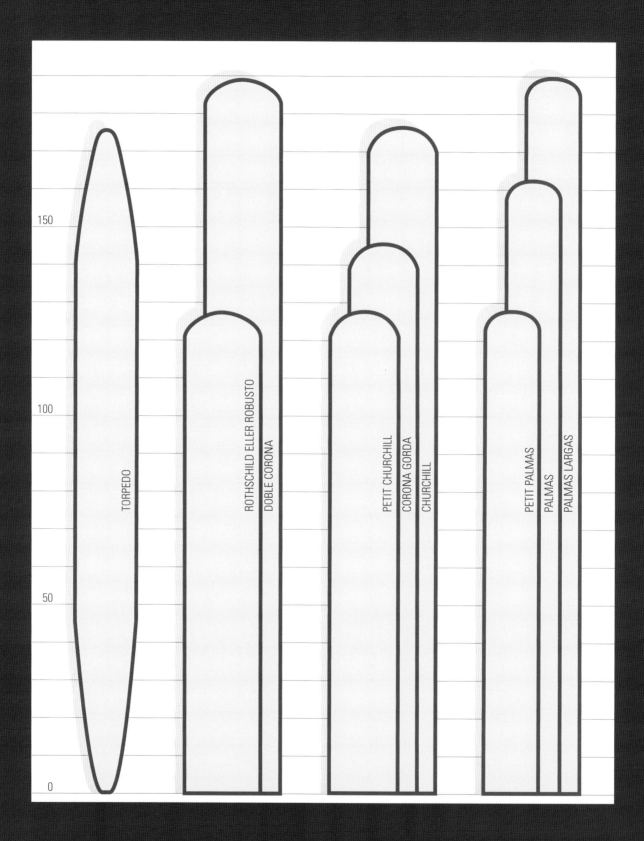

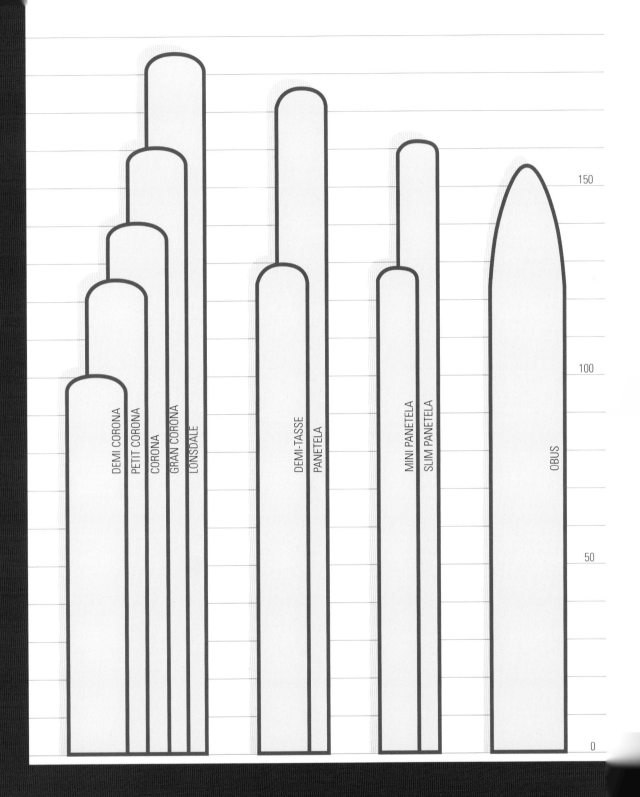

DEMI CORONA
PETIT CORONA
CORONA
GRAN CORONA
LONSDALE

DEMI-TASSE
PANETELA

MINI PANETELA
SLIM PANETELA

OBUS

150

100

50

0

Chapter V

A Pleasure beyond Description

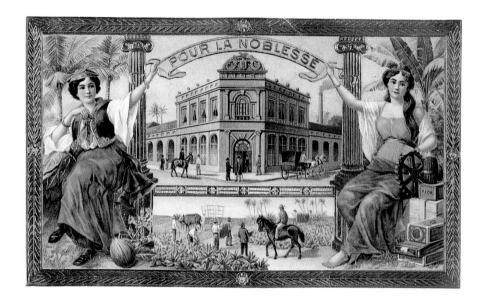

Eulogies on the cigar—here cigar equals the Havana, in the same way that Chambertin's praises may be sung but not those of *vin ordinaire*—would fill a huge library, in every language. Spanish is the first among them, as it should be. Diabolical or divine, the conquering tobacco of the conquistadors was celebrated in Castilian as soon as it was discovered. The classic writers of the Golden Age, led by Lope de Vega, often refer to snuff, pipes, and cigars, distinguishing between powdered and smoking tobacco. The first "made one sneeze," the second stimulated eloquence: "You take smoke in order to speak, after which you produce only vain wind," wrote Lope de Vega in *Amar, Servir y Esperar*. Less severe, one of the characters in *La Mayor Desgracia de Carlos V* suggests, "Take some tobacco, you'll cast off your care." Tirso de Molina, in *La Villa de Vallecas*, makes one of his characters mention a *tubano de tabaco* at the end of a meal, that is to say, a cigar, and why? To give a blessing—*Un túbano de tabaco/Para echar la bendición*—for it was customary in that Christian age to thank God when leaving the table.

Sixteenth- and seventeenth-century poets had recourse to mythology: tobacco must be the son of Proserpine and Bacchus, the goddess of the underworld and the god of drunkenness. "Divine Tobacco" wrote the English poet Edmund Spenser in *The Faerie Queene* in 1589. In 1598 Ben Johnson, in *Every Man in his Humour*, praised in tobacco "the most precious seed that the earth hath given to man." Tobacco is not mentioned at all in Shakespeare. It is one of the gravest reservations one can have about his works. At the beginning of the 17th century a rumor spread among poetry folk that the great Chaucer, author of *The Canterbury Tales*, who died in 1400, might have been able to sow tobacco on the slopes of Mount Parnassus. In his *Hymnus Tabaci*, published at Leiden in 1625, the poet Raphael Thorius a Torio had no doubts that smoking could make him "absorb God in my head." Molière, always decisive, makes Don Juan say, "Tobacco is divine, nothing equals it," "tobacco inspires feelings of honor and virtue," and "the man who lives without tobacco does not deserve to live." You would think that this was the last word on the subject. Not at all. A certain Cohausen saw in it "the king of the vegetable kingdom which reigns over the whole world," and amusingly adds that everywhere "the nostrils are its slaves." It is the companion of the prince at court and of the

Page 144:
Helmut Newton,
June with a Cigar.
Paris, 1962.

Following page:
Churchill cigars by
Romeo y Julieta set the
standard by which
others are judged.

peasant in the field, it accompanies the army on campaign and leads the muse to the writer's house.

Cuban poets never stopped celebrating it; for example, Diego García: "If sometimes my ideas are obscure/For they can be sometimes/The light of a cigar illuminates them/and my thoughts set off on their way." More recently, Guillermo

Charlie Chaplin in *Modern Times*, 1936.

Preceding page: Sir Winston Churchill painting in Madeira.

Facing page: Gary Cooper in Michael Curtiz's *Bright Leaf*, 1951.

Villaronda did not hesitate to maintain that "the cigar maker is a creator of dreams/Benvenuto Cellini of the leaf ..."! Cuban patriotism has always relied on tobacco. During the War of Independence, in 1895, Marcelo Salinas expressed things thus: "In every place where float/The bluish swirls/Of a cigar or a cigarillo/Rolled on Cuban soil/The Spirit is expressed/Of our Caribbean pearl." Villaronda, whom we have already quoted, wrote again, "Cuba is great and noble through its sweet-scented leaf/And this leaf is its second flag." All this is perhaps somewhat affected by poetic delirium, but tobacco itself makes one euphoric. Cuban quotations could be produced *ad infinitum*. Let us conclude this garland with

■

the three words of Che Guevara, who shows a completely modern and concrete sobriety: "Tobacco is ours."

Havana tobacco conquered Europe with the Romantic movement. Thus one should not be astonished at the warmth and emphasis of most of its partisans. In France, for example, Auguste Barthélémy and Jules Sandeau. The first, a satirical poet from Marseilles and creator with Méry of *Némésis*, a magazine attacking Louis-Philippe, declaimed in 1844 in his *Art de Fumer* [*Art of Smoking*]:

> *"It is necessary that the divine narcotic from Cuba*
> *Should lie heavy on my poetic couch with its blue swirls*
> *Cigars have often succeeded to my verses*
> *And I hope that this God will inspire these ones."*

Jules Sandeau is today one of the best-forgotten lovers of George Sand, with whom he wrote *Rose et Blanche* and then, on his own, *Mademoiselle de La Seiglière*, and finally, for the theater, with Émile Augier, *Le Gendre de M. Poirier* [*M. Poirier's son-in-law*]. He wrote in 1865:

"The cigar is found everywhere. It complements every idle and elegant life; every man who does not smoke is an incomplete man."

Cigar-box label, White Orchid.

Facing page: Orson Welles in his *F for Fake*, 1973.

Idleness and elegance go badly with poverty and even with being moderately hard up. For Sandeau the cigar could only be a Havana. Cigars were everywhere but were no better tolerated in society drawing-rooms than pipes. Women forbade each other to smoke them, by some strange inhibition or pure hypocrisy. Those most determined not to suffer any oppression would have none of this—they smoked with a vengeance: George Sand (perhaps she taught it to Sandeau during their brief liaison?); Marie d'Agoult, who gave up everything—husband, children, and reputation—in order to follow Liszt, himself an inveterate smoker of Havanas; the Princess de Metternich, the feisty wife of the Austrian ambassador to Paris; Rosa Bonheur, a painter and very prominent lesbian. These women, famous for a thousand reasons, their work, their loves, were also famous for their cigars. Without creating many followers. Should one rejoice at this? Or deplore the fact? It is a question that will continue to be asked.

Ridicule annihilated a number of eulogies at this time. Three years before Jules Sandeau a certain Chapus bravely published a *Manual for Well-Behaved Men and Women*—bravely, for lightly; his insights were uncertain, as was his style:

"At the time when the invasion of the cigar made itself felt in our habits of elegant life, about 30 years ago, women who at first had rebelled against the practice ended up by becoming far more than merely used to it. As soon as society ladies saw that they had been abandoned by fashionable young men, who carried their incense from Havana to the feet of parodies of duchesses, immediately the real duchesses, to rally the deserters, went as far as trying out cigars themselves. But they soon realized that this concession, like so many others, did not gain them a single inch of the disputed terrain, so they stopped and made short work of the cigar."

This strange text possesses only one merit: it bears witness to a powerful vogue. For the rest, it brings everything down: its author, the courtesans, duchesses, and Havana cigars. Had Chapus read Balzac, he would have learned that "real duchesses" considered themselves too far from their "parodies" to worry about borrowing whatever they liked from them, already sharing the essential thing with them—their sex—and distinguishing themselves from them by something superfluous—their rank—which made it unthinkable that they should be in competition with courtesans in anything at all, especially in love.

In Balzac we find as many cigars as duchesses. Among a thousand more solemn evocations of the same object, this energetic and trivial synthesis stands out which, better than some long speech, demonstrates to what extent the cigar had entered popular culture:

"For Christ's sake, I owe my tobacconist 30 francs for cigars and I dare not pass his accursed shop without paying for them."

Everything is summed up in these few words. Nothing could translate passion better than this indebtedness—30 francs was a lot under the July monarchy, especially for a young man up from the provinces, seeking to make his fortune. One only gets into debt for absolute things, ephemeral or eternal, trivial or transcendent ones. Property, apartments, automobiles, jewels, casinos, repayment of banker's loans … absolute banality! To get into debt for smoke is to take things to extremes, and a most singular expression of the absolute. But Balzac's best thoughts on cigars

Caricature by Jean Effel, *Paris Decked Out for Churchill*, 1945.

Facing page: Fujita in his studio in the Cité Falguière, Montparnasse. Paris, 1928.

Following pages: Preliminary interview for the book that François Truffaut was preparing on Alfred Hitchcock. Hollywood, 1962.

are expressed in the few lines which follow. The passage concerns the purest of his characters, with the hero of *Le Lys dans la vallée* [*Lily in the Valley*], Colonel Chabert, the miraculous escapee from the battle of Eylau who, carried off supposedly for dead, comes back from Germany several years later to discover that his wife has remarried with all his fortune and, though possessing every conceivable means of confounding the one and recovering the other, renounces the idea with absolute detachment.

It is at this moment that the lawyer Derville, another of Balzac's honest characters, decides to assist the colonel. He gives him some initial help, for Chabert hasn't a penny.

"When the colonel found himself in the street in front of a lamppost, he pulled from the letter the two twenty-franc pieces which the lawyer had given him and looked at them in the light for a moment. He was seeing gold again for the first time in nine years. 'So I am going to be able to smoke cigars,' he said to himself." Of all the laudatory utterances that the cigar has inspired, none has come anywhere near this one. Before Kipling in his *Fiancé* (1890), the Cuban poet García Nogueras, in his *Adele and Tobacco*, published in Havana in 1867, preferred cigars to his mistress.

The psychoanalyst Jacques Lacan, famous for the meanderings of his thought, smoked only twisted cigars of the *culebras* type.

Facing page: Twisted *culebras* cigars from Partagas and Romeo y Julieta.

Proust did not descend into these stereotypes. In *A la recherche du temps perdu* [*Remembrance of Things Past*], his Baron de Norpois, a diplomat worried by China and a perfect man of the world, throws his scarcely lighted Havana cigar on the gravel of the Avenue du Bois (now Avenue Foch) in order to be able to greet in due form a lady with whom he had a relationship. Here is a real sacrifice, despite its stupidity. This alone serves to elevate Proust above Kipling and Nogueras.

To complete a collection of texts which could go on for ever, here is an opinion

by the English humorist Jerome K. Jerome in *"On Being Idle,"* an essay in *Idle Thoughts of an Idle Fellow* (1889):

"Tobacco has been a blessing to us idlers. What the civil service clerks before Sir Walter's time found to occupy their minds with, it is hard to imagine. I attribute the quarrelsome nature of the Middle Ages' young men entirely to the want of the soothing weed. They had no work to do, and could not smoke, and the consequence was that they were for ever fighting and rowing."

Pierre Salinger.

Facing page: Jean Nouvel.

Following pages: Groucho Marx stretched out full-length, pretending to smoke a cigar.

CHAPTER
VI

OTHER CIGARS

August Sander, *Portrait of a Rhenish Peasant.*
Germany, ca. 1930–31.

production doubled, this sum would not be more than a tiny part of worldwide production of what are called cigars. So much the better.

"The world was created for a few"; the phrase is attributed to Caesar. Even had he never thought it, it would not be less striking, nor apparently less unjust, nor less

Kobke Christen Schjellerup (1810–48), *The Cigar Seller.*

deeply just. The vast majority of human beings have never drunk Château Petrus, and the number of the elect can only go on diminishing in view of the incomprehensible growth of the world's population. Petrus counts 11 hectares producing 45,000 bottles a year. The Vuelta Abajo region is 40,000 hectares and how many million *puros*? God alone knows, and perhaps the boardroom of Habanos S.A. The corresponding territories of the Dominican Republic, in the Yaque valley to the northwest of Santiago de los Caballeros—the best after the Vuelta, where production is treated with the same care—are of almost the same area. The limits are close. Those of the growth of mankind are not. Smokers of great cigars will always represent only a few of them.

■

Florida cigar bands from the Napoleonic era.

Everyone is free to join in or to deprive oneself of something else—cars, travel, clothes, a certain category of *objets d'art*, even books. Is the human condition not one of deprivation? Want is the lot of humankind. Now smoking makes one forget this. The only oblivion worthy of the name comes from smoke.

Love arouses more anxiety than the anguish it calms. Baudelaire said it all: "The panting lover leaning over his beauty/Looks like a dying man contemplating his tomb." Drink, so pleasant at first, hastens you into a daze, then delirium, and according to people who know about these things, the discomfort of the first is no less than that of the second. And so it goes on.

The derisory cigarette is already a cure for life's difficulties. The determination of millions of individuals—men and women—to take it up, despite all the health warnings and proof that it is harmful, bears abundant witness to the fact. What then can one say about the cigar?

The cigar is the supreme cure for such difficulties. It soothes the bad-tempered, calms the agitated, reassures the anxious, inspires dreamers, fortifies the weak—and there is no other side of the coin. Havana tobacco is not harmful. Abusing it is impossible; it satisfies without heaviness or regrets.

A great mystery remains and becomes even more insistent as the human race increases: why, for what reason, are cigar lovers so rare? For example, there appear to be around 50,000 in France, fewer than one Frenchman in a thousand. An astonishing minority.

The cigar lover, a fundamentally benevolent person because cigars make her so, only asks to share her passion, to multiply good will here below; it is not an unworthy

August Sander, *Portrait of a Young Countryman*.
Germany, ca. 1930.

Vetsch, telephoning cigar. Poster for Weber cigars (Weber Corona … *zieht besser*), 1959.
"Jovial" interpretation of the theme of the cigar-smoking boss.

Herbert Leupin, poster for Opal cigars, ca. 1950.
Herbert Leupin, poster for Rössli cigars, ca. 1960.

Cigars appropriate everything in the animal line. A spaniel watches over his master's *puros*. The gull accompanies them as they drift over the vast ocean. The pigeon, if a traveling one, could deliver them by air.

desire. Yet how often must she meet with refusal when offering a cigar to a possible new adherent she has identified? Ignorance perpetuates itself in ignorance. To deprive oneself voluntarily of an infallible means of escape from life's cares—though a depressing kind of courage—would be fairly impressive if the refuser were not giving up inestimable progress toward serenity, magnanimity, virtue. So the would-be donor puts her cigar case back in her pocket with the slight sadness, which a cigar will dispel, that once again she has witnessed a new proof of humanity's imperfection; together with, if she is not rich, the relief of retaining the *puro* which in her heart she has already given away. That is enough about the apparent injustice of Caesar's comment. That the world is made for a few does not mean that these few can do what they like with it. Caesar himself knew this only too well under Brutus's knife, but that they accepted him and agreed with him. Lovers of Havanas do not feel masters of the world when lighting up; quite simply, they get into phase with the best in the world, forming the closest alliance in history between nature and man, achieved with an American plant as go-between.

There is perfect agreement between the world and the smoker, for smoke—into which the cigar condenses and disappears, despite being such a rare product both by nature and manufacture, and increasingly becoming so, a product from a tiny fragment of the planet and those who cultivate it—is immaterial, intangible, and ephemeral. The first two attributes are divine, the third is the reverse side of eternity.

Cigar-box labels for Select, Wohl Bekomm's, and Castella cigars.

CHAPTER

VII

THE IMPORTERS

*F*acts: Almost all the cigars consumed in the world are smoked in Europe and the United States. Cigars smoked elsewhere, notably in Asia—with the exception of Burma—are smoked by Europeans. The buyers of cigars in airport duty-free shops, in particular, are all Westerners. As for importers, there are the official ones and the others. Apart from SEITA which, from the early 19th century to 1995, was controlled by the French state, half a dozen importers of top-of-the-range Havana and Dominican cigars share the best part of today's market of around six million cigars. The most important, in alphabetical order, are Belrive, Compagnie des Caraïbes, Coprova, Procigar, Soditab, and P & J Tobacco.

THE SOCIÉTÉ D'EXPLOITATION INDUSTRIELLE DES TABACS ET ALLUMETTES

*T*he import of cigars into France has been unrestricted since the end of the monopoly of SEITA, the former Service for the Industrial Exploitation of Tobaccos and Matches, heir of a royal monopoly which Napoleon had reestablished following its abolition during the French Revolution. The "Service" became a limited company (Société) in 1980 and a privatized company, still known as "SEITA," on 24 February 1995.

SEITA remains the number-one manufacturer and distributor of cigars in France, as well as of cigarettes and other smoking tobaccos. Its output covers all sections of the market, from great hand-rolled items to small cigars. Six hundred million SEITA cigars were sold in 1994, of which more than 95 percent were small ones (containing less than 3 grams of tobacco), i.e., a 40 percent market share. The bulk of the remainder is held by the Dutch, whose two leading brands are Henri Wintermans and Agio.

As cigar exporter, SEITA is number two in Europe.

Two things need to be made clear. First, the cigar market has been in decline for about twenty years on both sides of the Atlantic. Second, the average format of cigars smoked is also getting smaller. The two tendencies—market shrinkage, smaller cigars sold—are thus linked: the reduction in sales of big cigars has only

Germany and Belgium. The convergence of the price of small cigars and cigarettes resulted from a technological revolution, that of a spool mechanism, which permitted an increase in the speed with which the outer leaves of small cigars are formed, together with the relocation of certain factories in countries with low labor costs (SEITA has opened a branch in the Philippines). The spool process, whereby the cut-out wrapper and binder leaves are placed, without any form of glue, at 30 percent humidity, on cloth ribbons which are deep frozen in transit, has revolutionized the mechanical production of small cigars. Their production costs have stabilized, while the price of cigarettes has never stopped rising under the effect of increasing tax measures.

Cigarillo box, Cohiba Club Lights.

The great cigars, rolled by hand in Cuba since the beginning, and more recently in the Dominican Republic and Honduras, have never been consumed in great numbers. Their price would have been a limiting factor even if their relative rarity had not already determined the matter. Their consumption is also declining, and the general move toward smaller cigars immediately affected them. But the decline, strictly speaking, may also have resulted in part from the scarcity caused by a series of bad harvests in Cuba and judicial wrangling between the Castro regime and the exiled proprietors of the old trademarks which have been exploited by Havana.

Longchamp cigar box, Cuba tobacco.

In the mid 1980s France consumed between eight and nine million Cuban cigars, and fewer, 7.6 million, by 1991. By the mid 1990s only a little more than four million were smoked there. Beyond this figure, imports replenish stocks whose rotation will speed up, it is perhaps possible to hope, once the supply of sales points has been made certain. The chairman of SEITA, Jean-Dominique Comolli, did not rule out the possibility of the demand for top-of-the-range cigars in France reaching from ten to twelve million cigars per year.

The core component of luxury cigars, the big hand-rolled types, come from Cuba and the Dominican Republic.

SEITA's Pléiades range is produced for them in the latter country. This brand

Cigar-box label for Cadre Noir *panatellas*, a French brand of tobacco.

comprises thirteen types, of which 200,000 units per year are sold in France. SEITA exports many more—500,000 units in 1994—to the United States, the main recipient of Dominican production since the imposition of the Cuban embargo. (As a general rule, the Dominican Republic supplies the United States, and Cuba supplies Europe.)

Two agreements, one of 16 May 1994 and the other dated 14 March 1995, strengthened relations between SEITA and Havana. The first regulated payments on account intended to allow Cubatabaco to purchase equipment and supplies necessary for growing and manufacturing cigars on the island. In exchange Cubatabaco agreed to supply SEITA with 5,600,000 cigars. The following year this agreement was revised upward on 14 March 1995 in Havana. Cuba agreed to supply 6,179,000 cigars, of which 1,800,000 would be Montecristos, the Havana which is most sold in France (and the world).

SEITA directly imports the following brands: Bolívar, Cohiba, Hoyo de Monterrey, H. Upmann, Montecristo, Partagas, Por Larranaga, Punch, Quintero, Romeo y Julieta, and Quai d'Orsay. Their varieties are manufactured exclusively for the company in Cuba: in all, sixty-nine types of cigar, whose average sales price is around fifty francs.

Cigar boxes: Pléiades Orion (24 pack) and mini cigars.

The Belrive company is a wholly owned subsidiary of the Davidoff group, which is itself a subsidiary of the Oettinger firm; a very old company, the latter was based in Basel and has specialized in tobacco since 1875, when it was founded by Max Got. Bought by M. Huppuch in the 1930s, his son-in-law, Dr. Ernst Schneider, took over in 1961. Oettinger is the top Swiss tobacco company. The head office has more than 5,000 references available and supplies five distribution centers in the Confederation. Here a few words of history may be of use.

The Davidoff firm—a simple tobacco shop—was opened in Rue du Marché, Geneva, in 1911, by the father of the famous Zino, a Ukrainian emigré. Half a century later Zino was the king of Havana cigars in Europe and certainly the most famous cigar merchant in the world. It was to him that the Cubans turned for advice after the confusion resulting from Fidel Castro's victory in 1959 forcibly brought about a complete reorganization of the production and sale of *puros*. Yet this famous man had not yet reached the climax of his career. In 1969, at the age of

The Davidoff colonial mansion, Cuba.

Zino Davidoff, 1987.

62, he signed a contract with Cuba which authorized him to manufacture Havanas under his own name. That was glory indeed, but at the same time he dreamed of ensuring his succession; his only daughter, Sonia, who had married a Zurich doctor, was not really a candidate. The following year, 1970, Dr. Schneider convinced him to develop his brand on a worldwide scale, provided him with the means of doing so, and took back the famous label for Oettinger, having ensured that Zino would collaborate with him for five years.

Those five years went on for nearly a quarter of a century, until Davidoff died in Geneva in 1994. Twenty-five years of progress, with only one black mark, the quarrel with Cuba which occurred in 1989.

"During all that time they spent together," declares Raymond Scheurer, the deputy director-general of Davidoff International, "we tended the tree we had planted. And the tree has become a forest." Belrive is one of its most luxuriant thickets.

The turnover of the Davidoff group amounts to 670 million Swiss francs; it finances itself completely; it employs more than 1,650 people throughout the world, hand-picked by a process of internal training and promotion. "There are five selection criteria," jokes M. Scheurer, "and the four first are the same—attitude and state of mind, … attitude and state of mind—the last is competence."

Belrive was founded in 1974 on the initiative of Jacques Douce, then head of Havas and a passionate cigar lover, with the aim of bringing Davidoff products to France by including them in the SEITA catalogue. Zino Davidoff's famous shop was located at 2, rue de Rive, Zurich; and the choice of this head office was worth more than a mere wink. SEITA distributed Davidoff and Belrive on the proverbial shoestring, with two employees, until in 1989 Dr. Schneider decided to develop it. As a subsidiary company of Davidoff, Belrive had to promote the brand and develop its sales.

Toward the end of the 20th century, Belrive, French bridgehead of Davidoff International, possessed twenty-six of its own subsidiaries and owned thirty-five shops; its manager at the time was Patrice Greber. His twenty-six collaborators covered all French territory. They imported more than twenty brands of cigar from the whole world, excluding Cuba since the discord of 1989.

The Davidoff range of cigars is based on products made by hand in the Dominican Republic by the Kelner family. Nineteen models, including Aniversario 1 and 2; Davidoff 1, 2, and 3; Ambassadrice; five types of Davidoff Grand Cru; the series of 1,000 (five numbers); Davidoff Special "R," Double "R," and Special "T." "In the Dominican Republic we control everything, from seed to ash," insisted M. Scheurer.

Facing page: Cigar box, Davidoff, Special "R."

To the Davidoff cigars of the Dominican Republic should be added Belrive Sélection, six hand-made types of cigar, Señoritas to Double Coronas.

The Zino group, hand-rolled, came from Honduras. Launched with the American market in mind, cheaper than the Davidoffs (costing around three dollars each compared with fifteen for a Davidoff), it consists of four Mouton Cadet types and eight others. Other, somewhat lighter, Zino cigars are made with tobacco from Java, Sumatra, and Brazil.

In 1995 Belrive sold 530,000 hand-made cigars, 710,000 machine-made cigars, and more than 11 tons of smoking tobacco.

GÉRARD

*G*érard and Son, a Geneva firm, succeeded Davidoff in the incomparable role of master of the Havana cigar in Switzerland. The two Gérards are now only one since the older Gérard died in 1994. His son Vahé now holds on his own the flaming torch which they brandished together for thirty years. The company is now established in the foyer of the Noga Hilton, which makes the Quai des Bergues "a continuation of the Malecón"—to quote Arnould de Liedekerke—where the new Hotel Cohiba is the setting of one of the finest *puro* stores in Havana. Cigar sellers—and nothing but sellers—as well as lovers of pure cigars, the Gérards are proud to sell only Havanas, and the best ones possible. They have the fussiest customers in Europe.

Father and son used to go to Cuba every year to be present at the harvest and form an opinion on the qualities which would go into the manufacture of *puros*. Their name is attached to a range of mixed cigars, the "Gérard Selection" which only they sell, and that allows these great traders to count as importers.

All the boxes which arrive in Geneva are subject to a permanent control process which continues until they are sold: cigars are tested to check their state. Finally, having mentioned that Gérard and Son offer a range of large cigars—double *coronas* and beyond, which are normally unobtainable given the rarity of great wrapper leaf—it will be understood, we hope, that Vahé Gérard is one of the exceptional servants of the cult of Havana cigars.

Facing page: Bundle of 50 Havanas in a cigar cabinet. Cuba, 1995.

For a century Dunhill has been the greatest English name in tobacco. Alfred Dunhill, who founded the brand, started by selling chewing tobacco and pipe tobacco mixtures. The latter quickly established his reputation, as did his pipes with their famous white dot. Cigars followed. Dunhill, Winston Churchill's supplier, was for a long time the top Havana importer in the United Kingdom, with its shop at 30 Duke Street, equipped with a "maturing room," the temple of the art of smoking; and Alfred Dunhill's book, *The Gentle Art of Smoking* was the smoker's bible. Like Davidoff, Dunhill had its own brand of Havanas, launched in 1968 but discontinued in 1992 on account of insufficient distribution; its crowning achievement was the huge cigar known as the Havana Club, sold in a special box, analagous to the Montecristo A.

Today the famous old company has been taken over by Peter Stuyvesant, a giant in the tobacco world. Rothmans International is responsible for sales and for promoting all the tobaccos under the Dunhill name. The company's cigars are manufactured by hand by the Consolidated Cigar Corporation in the Dominican Republic, and by CITA at Tenerife in the Canaries.

The first-mentioned constitute the Dunhill Aged Cigar range, which comprises twelve types, from the Churchill to the very small Corona, of which three are sold in tubes (the Churchill Cabreras, the Tabaras *corona*, and the Rothschild Altamiras). The fillers are made of Brazilian tobacco, *piloto* and *olor*, the binder leaf is from the Dominican Republic, and the wrapper leaf from Connecticut. They are sold throughout the world.

The second, Dunhill Canary Island Cigars, are made in five types and are obtainable only in the United States. The fillers are from Brazil, the Dominican Republic *piloto seco* and *piloto ligero*, the binder leaf also from the Dominican Republic, and the wrapper leaf from Connecticut.

A third Dunhill range bears the name Dunhill European Range. It comprises three cigarillos, machine-made in Holland by Schimmpelninck using Bahia and Java tobaccos for the filler, Java leaf for the binder, and Sumatra leaf for the wrapper. A large Corona was launched in October 1996.

Naturally, Havanas are found in London, in Dunhill's sumptuous shop, which

CHAPTER VIII

ADVICE FOR SMOKERS

*H*ow to relight a cigar

"Relight a cigar?" you may murmur, "How vulgar and rather disgusting!" You are quite wrong. Of course, you shouldn't relight three-day-old ashes, but nothing should stop you—least of all considerations of good taste—from relighting the end of a cigar that you have absentmindedly allowed to go out.

All the same, you should first even up the end using a match-stick before continuing with the relighting process.

*H*ow to carry your cigars about

Just slip them into a cigar case.

Above: Jimmy "the Schnozz" Durante, Metro Goldwyn-Mayer.
Right: Cigar case with the initials H. A. M.
Facing page: Marcel Duchamp in his studio at Neuilly.

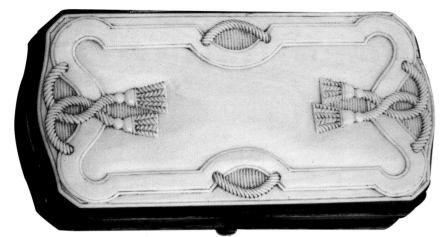

Cigar case with relief decoration imitating braided cords. Ivory, with pink satin interior. France, second half of 19th century.
Cigar case decorated with scene of women bathing. Ivory. France, second half of 19th century.
Cigar case decorated with humorous scene: a suitor leaves a woman at her window and is bitten by a dog as he tries to climb over a wall. Martin lacquer. France, ca. 1850.
Tobacco jar with polychrome decoration of tobacco leaves surrounding the word *Tabac*. Saint-Omer faïence with tin-plate screw lid. France, early 18th century.

Cigar case decorated with a bird on the lower half. Woven straw. France, end of 19th century.
Cigar case decorated with a fisherman carrying a net over his shoulder and holding a fish, set against a black background showing an inscription on the back: "Nice." Wood with marquetry decoration. Italy, 1930.

Cigar case to hold two *coronas*. Ends in black enamel with ribbed fillets, in polished yellow gold; outer cover in Russian leather with an applied crown. Cartier of Paris, 1929.

Cigar case dating from World War I.

THIS AIRTIGHT TIN
CONTAINS FIVE

La. Flor. de. Loreny

coronets

CIGARS
Selected and Packed
For Campaigning
By
ALFRED DUNHILL,
30, Duke Street,
SAINT JAMES'S, LONDON, S.W.

Leonard Briggs Esq.

"**A**rrived at that comforting conclusion, I bethought myself of a cigar and went below to get it. All was still down below. ... I came out again on the quarter-deck, agreeably at ease in my sleeping-suit in this warm breathless night, a glowing cigar in my teeth. ..." Peace, not a sound from men, things, or the elements, serenity, and the need for a secret comforter—all contribute to the unique nature of the moment of enjoyment of the captain to whom Joseph Conrad attributes these reflections in the opening pages of *The Secret Sharer* (1912).

Whether enjoyed alone or in company, a cigar demands your time, not the kind of time measured by a stopwatch, but the other, the timeless, which bears you into another world of dreams and reflections. The cigar does not require it to be night and can equally be satisfied by the post-lunch period, giving it an incomparable voluptuousness especially if the menu was not too Spartan. A cigar tastes better after an old-fashioned *ris de veau* than a burger and fries. Cigars require a suitable environment for their enjoyment, including soothing silence. One should never even think of smoking a cigar in a noisy street or of smoking two cigars in succession. A good cigar is an intense experience which would be ruined by repetition. Finally, while wind is the enemy of the smoker (they say it "eats and smokes" the *puro*), nothing should stop you smoking out of doors if the weather conditions are suitable and if you want to. The authentic smoker should observe three golden rules: light your cigar in a sheltered place, do not smoke while walking, do not inhale. The smoker should give smoke back to the air while enjoying its flavor.

Although they all bear first or second names which sound Spanish, these lithographs decorated cigar boxes in the United States. The dusky woman has always been one of the favorite themes of the creators of *vistas*.

BUTLERS THE CIGAR BAR
10th & H St. N.W.

FLORIDA

MIAMI

CASA JUANCHO
RESTAURANT
2436 S.W. 8th St.

HOTEL CASA DE CAMPO
2600 SW 3rd Ave., #300

LE PAVILLON RESTAURANT
AT THE HOTEL
INTERCONTINENTAL
100 Chopin Plaza

MORTON'S OF CHICAGO
1200 Brickell

SPEAKEASY-LES DEUX
FONTAINES AT THE OCEAN
FRONT HOTEL
1238 Ocean Dr.

MIAMI BEACH

CAFE ROYAL AT THE HOTEL
SOFITEL MIAMI
5800 Blue Lagoon Dr.

THE FORGE
432 Arthur Godfrey Rd.

I PAPARAZZI
940 Ocean Dr.

JIMMY AT CUBA CLUB
432 Arthur Godfrey Rd.

JOE'S STONE CRAB
227 Biscayne St.

THE LIVING ROOM AT THE
STRAND
671 Washington St.

YUCA
501 Lincoln

GEORGIA

ATLANTA

ATLANTA BEER GARDEN
3013 Peachtree Rd. NE

BELUGA'S MARTINI BAR
3115 Piedmont Rd.

CHEETAH CLUB
887 Spring St. NW

FILIBUSTER'S
1049 Juniper St.

THE FOX AND HOUND
1193 Collier Rd. NW

GOLDFINGER'S
3081 E. Sadowlawn NE

HAVANA CLUB
247 Buckhead Ave.

MAC ARTHUR'S
2171 Peachtree Rd. NE

THE MARTINI CLUB
1140 Crescent Ave.

OTTO'S CIGAR BAR
265 E. Paces Ferry Rd. NE

PEKASO'S
3167 Peachtree Rd.

PHOENIX BREWING CO.
5600 Roswell Rd.

PRINCE OF WALES
1144 Piedmont Ave.

THE ROSE AND CROWN
288 E. Paces Ferry Rd. NE

HAWAII

KAPOLEI

AZUL RESTAURANT
Ihilani Resort & Spa,
Ko'Olina Resort, 92-1001
Olani Street

HONOLULU

CAFFE PRONTO
131 Kauilani Avenue,

JOHN DOMINIS
RESTAURANT
43 Ahui Street

HILO

SHOOTER'S BAR & GRILL
121 Banyan Drive

NIHON RESTAURANT
123 Lihiwai St.

LOUISIANA

NEW ORLEANS

ARNAUD'S BAR
813 Bienville St.
LA 70112

MISSOURI

SAINT LOUIS

CARDWELL'S
8100 Maryland

DIERDORF & HART'S
STEAK HOUSE
323 Westport Plaza

KEMOLL'S OF ST. LOUIS
211 N. Broadway

LO RUSSO'S CUCINA
3121 Watson

RITZ-CARLTON
100 Carondelet Plaza

TONY'S
410 Market St.

WILBUR & GIL'S
633 West Port Plaza Drive

ST. CHARLES

EAGLE'S NEST CLUB
83 Charlestowne Plaza

CREVE COEUR

GROWLER'S PUB
763 Old Ballas

KANSAS CITY

AMERICAN RESTAURANT
25th & Grant

CAFE ALLEGRO
1815 W. 39th St.

JASPERS
405 W. 75th St.

MAJESTIC STEAKHOUSE
931 Broadway

BB'S LAWNSIDE
BAR-B-QUE
1205 E. 85th St.

SAVOY GRILL
219 W. 9th St.

MASSACHUSETTS

BOSTON

AMBROSIA ON
HUNTINGTON
116 Huntington Ave.

ANGELO'S
575 Boylston St.

BLACK GOOSE
21 Beacon St.

BLACK ROSE
160 State Street

CAFÉ VITTORIA
292 Hanover Street

COOGAN'S BLUFF
160 Milk Street

GREEN DRAGON TAVERN
11 Mashall Street

THE GOOD LIFE
28 Kingston Street

LA FAMIGLIA, THE
TREMONT HOUSE
275 Tremont St.

LEGAL-C BAR
Statler Office Bldg.
27 Columbus Ave.

NED KELLY'S
1236 Dorchester Ave.

PLAZA III
101 S. Market Bldg.
Faneuil Hall

REGAL BOSTONIAN HOTEL
9 Blackstone St.

YE OLDE UNION OYSTER
HOUSE
41 Union Street

THE VAULT BISTRO &
WINE BAR
Liberty Square

NEW YORK

NEW YORK CITY

1ST AVE.
361 1st Ave.

53RD ST. CIGAR BAR
53rd St. & 7th. Ave.

ALVA
36E. 22nd. St.

ANGELO & MAXIE'S
STEAKHOUSE
233 Park Ave. S.

BEEKMAN BAR AND BOOKS
889 1st Ave.

THE BUBBLE LOUNGE
228 W. Broadway

CAFE AUBETTE
119 E. 27th St.

CAMPAGNA
24 E. 21st St.

CARNEGIE BAR AND BOOKS
156 W. 56th St.

THE CIGAR ROOM AT
TRUMPETS AT THE GRAND
HYATT HOTEL
Grand Central Station

CINQUANTA
50E. 50th St.

CITY WINE & CIGAR CO.
62 Laight St.

CLUB MACANUDO
26 E. 63rd St.

COCO PAZZO
23rd E. 74th St.

DELANO DRIVE
RESTAURANT
E. 25th St. & the East River

FILLI PONTE RISTORANTE
39 Debrosses St.

FLORIO'S OF LITTLE ITALY
192 Grand St.

FLOWER'S
21 W. 17th St.

FRANKIE & JOHNNIE'S
269 W. 45th St.

GRAND HAVANA ROOM
666 5th Ave.

MARYLAND

BALTIMORE

BALTIMORE BREWING CO.
104 Albemarle St.

DA MIMMO FINEST ITALIAN
CUISINE
217 S. High St.

EDGAR'S BILLIARD CLUB
1 E. Pratt St.

THE FISHERY RESTAURANT
1717 Eastern Ave.

MAX'S ON BROADWAY
737 S. Broadway

SAVANNAH AT THE
ADMIRAL FELL INN
888 S. Broadway

MINNESOTA

MINNEAPOLIS

8TH STREET GRILL
Marquette Ave.

BRIT'S PUB
1110 Nicollet Mall

HYATT-REGENCY SPIKES
SPORTS BAR
1300 Nicollet Mall

J. D. HOYT'S
301 Washington Ave. N.

JAMES PAGE CIGARS &
HOMEBREW
2720 University S.E.

JAX CAFE
1928 University Ave. N.E.

MORTONS OF CHICAGO
555 Nicollet Ave.

ROCK BOTTOM BREWERY
800 La Salle Plaza

RUTH'S CHRIS
920 Second Ave. S.

TEXAS

HOUSTON

BIG JOHN'S
NEIGHBORHOOD BAR
6150 Wilcrest at Harwin

BRENNAN'S
3300 Smith St.

DOWNING STREET LTD.,
NO. 10
Kirby Oaks Center / 2549,
Kirby Dr.

Acknowledgments

The editor thanks Eric Deschodt and Philippe Morane, authors of the present work, as well as the photographers Patricia Canino, Karine Veyrunes, and Jacques Boulay.

He expresses his gratitude to Messrs. Jean-Dominique Comolli, chairman/managing director of SEITA; Raymond Scheurer, vice-chairman of Corporate Communication Davidoff; Roberto Yaech, Coprova; and José Maria Cases, Franc-Port S.A.

His sincere thanks are due to all those who contributed to the production of this book: Marie-Claire Adès, conservator, SEITA gallery and museum; Carlos Amado Blanco, general manager of Intertabak A.G.; Antoni Armengol Vila, La Casa del Tabacs, Andorra; Emmanuel d'Arthuys; Geneviève Barachon, Coprova; Patrick Benoist, Area director, Western Europe Tabacalera, France; Louis-Gérard Biret, Casa del Habano, Paris; Daniel Campion, marketing and sales director, SEITA; Simon Chase, Hunters & Frankau, London; Teresa Conesa Fabregues, public relations director, Tabacalera, Madrid; Nicholas Freeman, Hunters & Frankau, London; Vahé Gérard, director, Gérard Père et Fils, Geneva; Patrice Gréber, director, Davidoff, France; Fritz Maeder; Danielle Masson, archivist, SEITA gallery and museum; Helmut Newton; Eric Nussbaum, conservator, Cartier Collection, Geneva; Isabelle Ockrent, public relations director, SEITA; Françoise Pace; Marcelle Piaulet; Liliane Sabatini, conservator, Walloon Museum, Liège; Antoinette Schmied, conservator, Pipe and Tobacco Museum, Lausanne; Howard Smith, conservator, Dunhill Museum, London; Alice Springs; Jean-Michel Tardy; Véronique Van de Ponseele, conservator, Museum of Natural History, Paris; Luc Vercammen, director-general, Établissements Suter; Bruno Vuaille, director, cigar division, SEITA; and Norbert Wiedmer.

Photographic Credits

Arnaud Baumann: 162, 163: The Bettmann Archive: 24, 129; Bibliothèque Centrale du Muséum National d'Histoire Naturelle, Paris: 21; Bibliothèque Nationale Estampes: 17, 23, 25, 30, 31, 70, 77, 157; Bibliothèque Forney, Paris: 3, 50, 107, 109, 107, 109, 135, 146, 172, 174, 175; Vatican Library: 28, 29; Jacques Boulay: jacket, 2, 64, 86, 94, 136, 181, 182, 183, 187, 202; Bridgeman-Giraudon: 61, 97; Patricia Canino: 6, 7, 8, 9, 53, 57, 60, 143, 148, 193, 216; Cahiers du Cinéma Colección: 153; Antigua Cartier Collection, Ginebra: 208, 209, 211, 215; Christophe L. Colección: 150, 151, 155; Wallace Collection, London: 61; Copyright Archives/matthieu Prier: 205; Dr: 10, 19, 25, 38, 39, 43, 73, 82, 83, 87, 90, 91, 102, 137, 152, 190, 203, 220; Alfred Dunhill Archive Collection, London: 99, 199, 200, 206, 209, 211, 212, 215; Gallery Tretiakov, Moscow: 97; García/Davidoff Ettinger: 185; Gavin Graham Gallery, London: 51; Sr. Gérard: 196; Giraudon: 77, 104, 105; N.P.G.-Giraudon: 65; Patrick Glaize: 12, 114, 115; Iürg Hafen, Bern: 116, 118, 184; A. Kertesz/Ministry of Culture (France): 156; The Kobal Collection: 164; Lauros-Giraudon: 32, 33, 51, 78; Magnum Photos: 88, 89 (Burt Glinn/Magnum), 93 (René Burri/Magnum), 95, 158, 159 (Philippe Halsman/Magnum), 213 (Cartier Bresson/Magnum); Museum of Walloon Art, Liège: 37, 40, 41; Musée Carnavalet, Paris: 70, 74, 78; Musée Orsay, Paris: 32, 33; Musée de la Pipe et Objets du Tabac, Lausanne: 218; Musée Toulouse Lautrec, Albi: 77; Félix Nadar/Caisse Nationales Des Monuments Historiques et des Sites: 48, 69, 71, 72; National Portrait Gallery, London: 65; Helmut Newton: 144; Réunion des Musées Nationaux: 171; Roger-Viollet: 70, 74, 75, 149; Maurice Rougemont/Agence Gamma: 161; August Sander: 91, 170, 173; Musée de la Seita, Paris: 5, 7, 14, 15, 16, 20, 26, 27, 31, 34, 35, 36, 42, 43, 44, 45, 46, 47, 49, 52, 54, 55, 56, 58, 59, 62, 63, 66, 67, 68, 76, 79, 80, 81, 84, 92, 96, 98, 133, 134, 154, 160, 167, 168, 174, 175, 177, 180, 183, 204, 207, 208, 209, 210, 211, 214, 217, 218; Karine Veyrunes: 100, 101, 106, 108, 111, 114, 115, 116, 117, 119, 120, 121, 122, 123, 124, 125, 126, 128, 130, 131.